D1087481

CHOOSING SIDES

Playground and Street Life on the Lower East Side

Cary Goodman

with a Foreword by Stanley Aronowitz

SCHOCKEN BOOKS • NEW YORK

First published by Schocken Books 1979

Copyright © 1979 by Cary Goodman

10 9 8 7 6 5 4 3 2 1   79 80 81 82

First Edition

Library of Congress Cataloging in Publication Data

Goodman, Cary.
  Choosing sides.

  Bibliography: p.
  Includes index.
  1. Sports—Social aspects—New York (City)—History.
2. Play—Social aspects—New York (City)—History.
3. Lower East Side, New York.   4. New York (City)—
Social conditions.   I. Title.
GV706.5.G66   301.5'7   79-12665

Manufactured in the United States of America

To My Family and Friends

Contents

Foreword

by Stanley Aronowitz

The rise of the sports metaphor in American life is among the most significant cultural developments of our age. The ubiquity of the metaphor may now have reached the point where sports is *the* metaphor for what we mean by American life. Corporations devise "game plans" for beating their competitors or selling their products; game theorists dominate policy planning for a myriad of government agencies. Indeed, the whole "science" of public choice economics is predicated on the assumption that once the objectives of policy are known, the rest is all a matter of working out the options in terms of various games. From politics, advertising, law, and public relations to the deadly game of war, we are drawing our images, our language, and our whole concept of strategy and tactics from the football field, the chess board, or other competitive sports. And it's all about winning. Perhaps jogging may be viewed as the one athletic activity which is not motivated by the criterion of victory. Yet even here, in this most seemingly noncompetitive of sports, the general goal of "good health" may be translated as an effort to "beat" old age, death—in short, to outrun time. We seem unable to avoid the encounter with an opponent, even if the adversary is history. Thus, the preoccupation with the spatial, the map, the field, is supplemented by the repetitive character of the game, its circularity; the rules serve to obliterate the historical, that inevitable temporality which overcomes even the most effective cosmetic, that game of illusion in which time is mystified.

In our culture aging becomes a "problem" to be solved by the subterfuge implied by the game-like quality of everyday life, its repetition, its habitual character. Our culture's remarkable capacity for forgetting is abetted by the translation of every human activity into sport. For the game is the representation of circularity—we "play" a round of golf, we make life into a game of roulette by watching ourselves perform our rounds—the repetition of a certain ordered discourse or routine intended to solve the same problems, the most significant of which is the problem of progression which has the force of disintegration. Our sports life is linked to the project of integrating everything into the circle of the game.

In a world in which everything is reduced to a "problem" subject to technological solution, the notions of "moves," of strategies—in short, of the manipulation of spatial relations—seem to dominate our thinking. The game has become self-referential; although its rules are consonant with some external constraint such as the requirement that the "bottom line" of profit be the canon of accountability for deciding whether the game is being played right, it enjoys autonomy at the operational level. Its results are assumed to be the outcome of having all the players lined up properly, as well as making the right moves on the battlefield. Battle plans are concocted to achieve certain goals. Even though the goal determines the way in which the game is played, the players get lost in the process, as if the goal flowed from the game and not the other way around.

Until Cary Goodman's book, most of us had no idea of how the activity of play, traditionally associated with the moment of freedom, either childhood or that portion of the day devoted to "what we will," was transformed into organized sport. Goodman succeeds admirably in showing the historical roots of the subversion of autonomous play by organized play and sport. By showing how time and space are categories of power, how their colonization by the liberal institutions of social work and recreation at the turn of the twentieth century was animated by more than philanthropy, Goodman goes a long step toward penetrating our taken-for-granted world. Perhaps the most important achievement of this book is to remind us that every aspect of our social existence has a history, that it came into being and is not just "there." By taking apart the sports metaphor and showing its political and social origins in processes of social struggle, particularly the antagonisms between labor and capital, he suggests that we may be able to recapture our own heritage. I mean the society of kids, the underworld that is the streets, that part of us that hides in school washrooms, engages in peer interaction in empty sandlots littered with broken glass, and plays for fun rather than profit.

Organized sports is an activity performed by players who are hired to entertain us, to help us pass the hours that would otherwise lie heavily on our backs, consistent with the law of the "bottom line." For many of us it is the way that we attain *involvement* in a world where the public sphere has become either fragmented or corrupted and forces a retreat into the privacy of our homes or the collective privacy of the stadium. For others it fills the spaces left vacant by the passing of material ambition and of the childhood keeping our fantasy life alive and well. But it is a spurious activity, a pale echo of a time when play was autonomous, when it was the very sign of a culture of resistance for both children and working people who made their own recreation, who knew how to entertain themselves.

In Goodman's rich documentation we learn that the power of the cultural and business apparatuses is not absolute. Its compulsion to overcome those autonomous working-class precincts that inhabited the Lower East Side of New York was intimately tied to the requirement that labor be degraded by cleansing the work process of its play elements on the one hand, and making play itself subject to the routinization introduced by organized sports.

Goodman also shows the way in which the mind–body split inherent in the assumptions of organized sport became a feature of that degraded labor. Characteristic of the author is his optimism that degradation is by no means an irreversible process. The last chapter is written in accordance with the principle of hope because it offers a program for change. Thus does Goodman depart from the conventions of the mere sociologist of sport who might rest content with the achievement of exposure or the glories of analytic reason. By situating dichotomy of sport/play in a specific historical context, rather than in the vagaries of human nature, by going *inside* the structures of our cultural life, Goodman points a way out. This feature of *Choosing Sides* distinguishes the work from either narrative histories that tell the story without drawing conclusions, or from sociological treatments that refuse the partisanship that is implied by the book's title. Goodman insists on placing the story of the organized-sports movement in its political and economic context in order to draw significance from that history for our own days. By linking this particular context to the larger context of the work/play separation, we are forced to address a set of issues that bear on our own lives. Goodman has done nothing less than demonstrate that speaking about sports is a way of speaking about daily life. If the workplace is the scene where the body is merged with the machine, the sports world is the site of the mechanization of the mind, its transformation from a speculative organ to an instrument. For sports is not merely exercise; it has become a way toward domination of techniques over both the mind and the body. The transition from autonomous play to organized play and sports is the switch from the notion of *abandon*, where body and mind range freely in time/space, to the rigorously enforced game rules that control body and mind, regimenting them to the iron cage of military and industrial disciplines. Sport is the place where we learn how to conform, how to repress our sexuality, how to jettison our childhood. We learn not to cry, to displace our protest by either "getting" the opponent or punishing ourselves. In Goodman's critique we get a glimpse not only of what ought to be, but also of what once was and can be again.

Preface

Growing up is never easy, but for some it's more difficult than for others. If you're poor, it's harder. If you're a stranger in a new land, it's harder. If you're poor and a stranger and derided as coming from a different, inferior stock, it's harder still. The sons and daughters of the immigrant masses who flocked to America around the turn of the century lived these dilemmas—of poverty, strangeness, and discrimination—day by day. They worked when other children played or went to school. They walked by others with full bellies while their own stomachs grumbled. They hurt inside as other children laughed. But they too survived, fashioning their own world of stale bread where baseball was played with an old sock or where the national anthem included a refrain that went "Oh say can you see/any bedbugs on me?" Their world was a counterworld within which they controlled meaning, mores, and tempo. The center of this counterworld was the streets.

Our grandparents lived and laughed and loved and grew to adulthood in the streets. The streets provided opportunities for community, kibitzing, and recreation. At the same time, the streets were centers of political action where soapboxers and strikes were a part of everyday life. In the streets, people struggled, loved, organized, and played, surrounded by familiar smells, sounds, people, and symbols. This book is about the streets and people of the Lower East Side of New York City during the years 1890–1914. It is about the destruction of an immigrant, working-class street life accomplished through various means—not the least of which was the rise of organized play and the movement for social reform of which it was a major part. It is about the childhoods of my grandfather or your grandmother, of people like Judith Levine.

Judith was born in 1902 in Austria-Hungary and came to America with her parents, two sisters, and a brother, at the age of two. She lived with them and assorted other relatives and boarders in a kosher home on East Fourth Street in the Jewish quarter of New York City. While her sisters worked as milliners and her brother served an apprenticeship to a watchmaker, Judith attended public school at P.S. 113, helped her mother around the house, and played jump rope, potsie, fox 'n geese, and other games on the streets and sidewalks of her block. Like most of her friends and neighbors, Judith was too poor for the "finer things in life" like new clothes, ice cream, or toys, so she made do with what she had and wished for what she didn't have. She remembers the having and the hoping and the experiences of her childhood that informed the two:

> I remember 1907 was a terrible panic. I was five years old and it seemed like almost every day we were feeding another, different boarder who never had the money to pay.
> From what was discussed, I think I remember that I knew that the boss is bad, the workers are good, and the union was good for them.

Seventy-five years later Judith remembers little incidents that, taken together, compose the texture of that place and time. About her native tongue she recalls, "I thought you were inferior if you spoke Yiddish." About school she says, "I loved to go to school; the teacher always told me, 'You mustn't guess, you must think.' But, the boys didn't like it there. When they spoke to the teacher they had a sort of sing-song tune. For them, the teacher was like police, the enemy." She had her own enemies, as well as friends. Once when she was playing hopscotch in the street, "A bicycle man ran me down. Instead of helping he yelled at me for playing in the street. I was on the ground looking up at this well-dressed man through his bicycle like through a chicken coop, hating my lecturer. I never saw him before or after."

Judith's friends, like Chassier Cherkofsky or a boy named "Flattie," came from her block, not from the organized institutions like the Educational Alliance or vacation playgrounds. "You stick in front of your house," she recalls, "you have adventure." She went to "her friend's roof" or sat on her stoop or went to Tompkins Square Park, which was "a very important part of my life." When she went to places like the vacation playground, the rhythm of her life changed:

> It wasn't unpleasant; it wasn't boring. You just killed time. It was someplace to go, something to do with hundreds of children. I didn't make any friends there, but I didn't feel bad about it.

At the Educational Alliance which Judith sometimes attended for an outing or to escape the winter's bitter chill, there was also an atmosphere of restraint, organization, and refinement that contrasted sharply with street culture:

> They [the Educational Alliance people] were the German Jews that were ashamed of us. They thought they could iron out the differences and make us all Protestants. They wanted a nice, refined religion. Bloodless.

These two different worlds—the worlds of the street and of organized play—are the subjects of this book. In a sense, there are two stories to be told, two voices to be heard, two directions to be charted. The first story comes from the thoughts and recollections of the immigrants themselves. It is a story rich with pathos and humor and one for which I am deeply indebted to those veterans of the Lower East Side at the turn of the century who shared their memories with me. I wish to thank Judith and Ben Levine, Charles Stein, Lilian Skupsky, Falk Sherman, Morris Mikelbank, Clara Hooper, Mina Lustfeld, Freida Cohen, Morris Gershfeld, and Isidore Kanowitz for taking the time to educate a "greener" about the period. For directing me to these friends and in appreciation of the wonderful work they do with senior citizens in the New York Jewish community, I wish to thank Project Ezra. For the financial and intellectual support that they provided me as I tried to discover immigrant history I owe a tremendous debt of thanks to YIVO, and most especially to Yadja Zeltman and Deborah Dash Moore, who were among the first to receive my ideas for this inquiry with support and enthusiasm.

In addition to speaking with these former Lower East Siders and reading the biographies and autobiographies of others, I gained some valuable insights into the everyday lives of the immigrants by first learning and then reading some Yiddish sources such as the *Jewish Daily Forward, Undzer Gezunt* ("Our Health"), and books and pamphlets published by the Workmen's Circle. For teaching me enough of my *mamaloschen* (mother tongue) to be able to undertake such an endeavor, I am grateful to Clara Lapan of the Columbia University–YIVO summer program in Yiddish studies.

In order to listen to the voices of the other world, the world of organized play, it was necessary to rely completely on printed sources since the leaders of the play movement have long since died. Here my efforts were assisted by the staff of the Rare Books Division of the New York Public Library; Roger Lancaster of the National Parks and Recreation Association, and the library staffs at Columbia University who allowed me to work with the Phelps Stokes papers; and at YIVO, by Marek Webl the YIVO archivist.

The general support I received in the conceptualization and shaping of this book came from some truly good friends, comrades, and scholars. I wish to thank Colin Greer of Union Graduate School for his efforts in teaching me the subtlety and complexity of immigrant life. I wish to thank Roy Fairfield, also of U.G.S., for his confidence in me while I was researching this book. My thanks also to Phil Shinnick of Rutgers University and Sports for the People for his help in decoding the messages of play and sport. My appreciation to Mark Naison, Paul Hoch, Mike Jay, Linda

Gonzalvez, Tom Karlson, Carlos Garcia, and other members of Sports for the People for the assistance and support they rendered in this effort. I owe a debt of gratitude to my dear friend Andrew Irving for his initial editing of this text, and to Léon King for his final editing and patience with a first-time author. Finally, a separate note of gratitude to Stanley Aronowitz of the University of California at Irvine, for the invaluable theoretical direction he gave me and for the critical reading he gave this manuscript in its varied forms.

I wish to thank my grandfather, Max Weidenfeld, for keeping the memory of the Lower East Side alive for me and my family. I wish to thank my parents, Roz and Sy Goodman, for the love and encouragement they've always given me; my sister Randy for her love, interest, and support; and Diane De Mauro, who was my constant source of comfort, assistance, love, and friendship during the time of this book's birth.

While I received an overwhelming amount of aid in forging the ideas of this book and in shaping its contents, the final burden of its errors rests solely with me.

Cary Goodman

Introduction

When you thought about Jews before 1880, you thought about a people very different from those who arrived in America after that date. You thought mainly about German Jews, about a small community with a large group of white-collar workers. In all of the United States with its 50 million inhabitants, there were only 250,000 such Jews. Some had come to America with the first colonists; most came in large waves of German emigration which took place in the middle of the nineteenth century.[1] Fifteen percent of the German Jews were brokers, bankers, company officials, and wholesalers; twelve out of every hundred were salesmen, collection agents, and auctioneers; 17 percent were accountants, bookkeepers, clerks, and copyists; while five out of every hundred were of the professional class.[2] The German Jews of America spoke English, treated Judaism as a faith rather than as a world view, and were almost thoroughly integrated into the mainstream of the American Way of Life.

For the years 1880 through 1910, when one thought about the Jews it was about an entirely different group of people. This was the period of a vast immigration of Jews from Eastern Europe. These Jews were the refugees of pogroms and poverty and they came to the United States with hopes and in numbers far beyond the wildest dreams of the German Jews already here. Between 1881 and 1890, 193,000 of these Yiddish-speaking Jews landed in America, mostly at Castle Garden; and, from 1891 to 1900, 393,000 more passed through the newly opened "Isle of Tears" (Ellis Island) in New York Harbor. From 1901 through the first ten years of the century, 976,000 Russian, Rumanian, Polish, Slavic, and Austrian Jews immigrated here.[3] Thanks to the arrival of these immigrants, by 1910 the Jewish population in the United States was "larger than in any country in the world, and New York had become the seat of the world's largest Jewish community."[4]

At the beginning of this mass immigration from Eastern Europe, leaders of the German-Jewish community—men like financier Jacob Schiff, attorney Louis Marshall, and philanthropist Felix Warburg—said, "We are not happy, but if small numbers are to be welcomed it should be young, skilled workers."[5] As the numbers of immigrants increased (from 5,692 in 1881 to 76,373 only twelve years later), the German-Jewish community reacted with dismay. Although more than a third of the newcomers were skilled laborers, many of those who came were poor. They spoke Yiddish, the mamaloschen (mother tongue) which the Germans considered jargon; they dressed like Europeans, not Americans; and they were forever taking to the streets with their grievances. They evoked such epithets as "clannish," "anarchist bombthrowers," "disease-infested," "feeble-minded," and more. The prospect that these Eastern European refugees might contribute to anti-Semitism by giving the Jew a bad name horrified their decorous co-religionists. The immigrants and their world became the object of a massive campaign funded by the German Jews and implemented by an emerging corps of social reformers. The campaign was called "Americanization."

The great majority of East European Jews settled on the Lower East Side of New York. In that congested district south of Fourteenth street and east of the Bowery, they evolved a thriving culture and a vast number of communal institutions to help them make the transition into

America. And if the district was not the land of milk and honey they had dreamed of before setting out from their homes in the *shtetln* and the cities of Europe, neither was it filled with pogroms and persecutions. For these strangers in a strange land the Lower East Side was an exciting ever-changing, noisy, emotion-filled "counterworld" where hopes, dreams, anxieties, and even the mundane were acknowledged and easily understood within familiar settings.

Many different types of institutions serving different sectors of the community developed side by side. For adults who wanted to combat the loneliness and isolation of life in a big city in the new world there were the *landsman-schaftn.* These mutual aid societies based on descent from the same towns or villages in Eastern Europe provided Jewish immigrants with loans, medical care, insurance, burial benefits, and the warmth of familiarity. If the *landsmanschaftn* were havens where the immigrants could assert the commonplaces of everyday life without fear of rebuke from the powers that be, then the Yiddish stage was a forum where everyday life could be openly ridiculed and the powerful excoriated. The Yiddish theater was a lively force for the political education of Jewish workers. It served as a people's library instead of mere entertainment. The vitality and ambivalences of the immigrants' experiences found opportunities for expression, assessment, and reflection through the theater where the intensity of life on the Lower East Side was examined.[6]

Examination of the problems faced by the Jewish immigrants was forthcoming not only from the stage but also from the Yiddish press and from the leaders of the immigrants themselves as they mounted soapboxes on their street corners and let fly against capitalism, sexual ignorance, exploitation, and the like. The Yiddish press which consisted of five major dailies with a circulation by 1915 of over half a million[7] was perhaps the most extensive of the counterworld institutions, but it was only one vehicle of ethnic and political information. Soapboxes were another.

Soapboxers could be found dotting the streets of the Lower East Side throughout the year—at Union Square, on

Rivington Street, in front of a factory, or at a busy interchange, but they were especially prevalent around election time. An orator would carry his (and sometimes her) wooden platform to a strategically significant location, plop down the box, mount it, and let fly with a vitality matched only by the religious revivalists or missionaries. Not only was there a certain *chutzpadik* quality to the concept of soapboxing, there was also a great educative role that the orators could and did play in bringing news about contemporary issues straight into the heart (and minds) of the community.

The issues were many, running the gamut from too much work to too much sickness, from too many mouths to feed to too many debts to pay. It was as if the immigrants were trapped in the gap between their desires and the false promise of America; the institution of soapboxing grew up to fill that gap with interpretation. Some of the interpretations were spellbinding, others were sarcastic, and most were pointedly simple. Many of the interpreters were anarchists, many were feminists, and most were Socialists of one stripe or another. But regardless of the differences in their ideologies, the soapboxers shared a common task—to gather and articulate a cogent political position in response to the bosses and the capitalist system that kept the bosses rich and often made the immigrants' next meal problematic. This task they pursued at many varied times and many different places.

Being a soapboxer was sometimes a dangerous task— Tammany goons would bust up Socialist rallies; Socialists sometimes attacked anarchists. In addition to the trait of fearlessness, the job of being a soapboxer required many other skills and abilities. It called for a working knowledge of social psychology and politics, a good voice, and a clear head. A Socialist paper of the period, in an article addressed to street-corner orators, stated succinctly both their task and the requisite talents:

> Your main object at the street corner being to set the mental gums of your crowd going...genuine street cornerism adjusts to the community and the crowd; develop your public voice....What you shall say is by no means the primary consideration; but can you say it soapboxly.[8]

Saying it "soapboxly" meant saying it with a passion. Samuel Chotzinoff, a chronicler of the period, remembers his lessons in front of a Socialist soapboxer:

> I would often join the small crowd in front of one of these men and listen to descriptions of soul-and-body-destroying sweatshops and impassioned enumeration of the inequities of the "bosses" who owned them. . . . I heard with horror that the "bosses" were drinking the blood of their workmen and women. And while I knew that to be only a figure of speech (my mother often accused me of drinking hers) the image it evoked gave me the measure of soulless cupidity of the possessing class. . . .[9]

These street-corner orators were the bards of the boulevards, singing songs of sadness and telling tales of optimism, of messianic days ahead, once the doctrine of socialism (or anarchism or feminism) had come to replace the capitalist social order. But the combined assault of mass culture in the rise of the radio and the repressive anti-free-speech tactics that were used by state and local militia worked to destroy the influence and importance of soapboxers. Charles Stein, who lived on the Lower East Side, remembers going to hear Eugene V. Debs, and Lilian Skupsky, who grew up there, went out to listen to the oratory of Morris Hillquit and Meyer London. Ben Levine, a veteran listener, recalls that the soapbox speakers "were very fascinating and very able": "They made socialism down to earth, community talk about prices, working conditions, you know. . . . I think they made a lot of converts to socialism."[10]

Not all the institutions of the Jewish quarter were as solemn and serious as soapboxing, as sex segregated as the *landsmanschaftn*, or as meaningful as the Yiddish stage. Some were mainly just for fun. In this category there were the candy stores, or "Cheap Charlies" as they were called. These small stores, where children and youth gathered to talk over boxing and baseball or boyfriends, dotted the Lower East Side. The candy store, like the *landsmanschaftn* hall, was a meeting place for gossip, a card parlor, and a haven for the jokes and jibes of East European folklore. In addition to the candy stores there were the cafes where politics, literary criticism, and mainly kibitzing came with a nickel's investment in tea leaves and hot water. One immigrant described the cafes as places of unbridled levity and passion where "people feel free, act independently, speak as they think and are not ashamed of their feelings."[11] As Harry Roskolenko, a veteran chronicler of the period, put it, the cafes "were the living centers of a liquid culture flowing from the earnest immigrant's soul."[12]

Part of that flow was music, which in its various forms— street organs, dance halls, and balls—constituted an institution of its own right in the community. Bella Mead, researching her master's thesis at Columbia University in 1904, walked along the streets of the Lower East Side cataloguing the "Social Pleasures of the East Side Jews." She found that within the three blocks from Grand to Clinton Streets, there were posters advertising at least nineteen different balls and entertainments. The sidewalks of the district she described as "an impromptu dance hall."[13]

Music was everywhere, filling the air and the cracks between the cobblestones. For the young women of the neighborhood, dancing to the tunes of the street fiddler was a major source of entertainment. The University Settlement noted the importance of dancing in a report issued in 1901: "For the girls, the street organs supply the excitement which their brothers get from the fires....And every time they grind out a tune the girls gather round and dance.[14] Stepping and swaying to the music of the organ grinder offered these young women, many of whom did "double duty" as wage earners and mothers or mother's helpers, a respite from the tedium of sewing in seams and the monotony of the factory milieu. Like the dice games engaged in by their male counterparts, it provided a social setting wherein they might discuss working conditions or gossip, share recipes or heartfelt needs, dream, escape, and exercise. In part, music and dancing were compensations for the oppression of everyday life. Lilian Skupsky has fond memories of dancing and the dance halls of the district:

> I was a very good dancer and I used to go on Friday, Saturday, or Sunday night. I would go with a group of girlfriends and that's how I met my husband....We used to dance the fox-trot and ballroom dancing. The first time I

went, I didn't know anything about dancing except the
Virginia reel and things like that....After a while, I learned
how to dance and I loved it....When I went to work, I
didn't have much time for dancing.[15]

Other women had other experiences that were less joy-
filled because the dance halls on the Lower East Side were
of many types. Some were connected to a saloon; some were
rented by procurers, who tried to (and did, in some cases)
lure young girls into "white slavery" (prostitution); and
some were run by shysters quick to make a profit off the
anxiety of girls eager to Americanize their leisure habits.
The proprietors of such halls, who rented them at inexpen-
sive rates (thirty-five dollars per month for use on week-
nights), cared less about the fox-trot than they did about
the opportunity to realize a fast buck. But despite the
periodic scandals involving charges of prostitution that
emerged about one of the halls, or academies as they were
sometimes called, and despite the zealous efforts of
reformers to close down all the halls, they survived. Mainly
that was because most of the halls were neither fronts for
prostitution nor rip-offs—they were simply places to which
one could escape, and enjoy. They were a part of immigrant
culture no less so than the cafes and the Cheap Charlies.
Indeed, because the dance halls were one of only a few
institutions that serviced both males and females, one
could even make the case that they were of prime
importance.

This counterworld—of *landsmanschaftn,* Yiddish theater
and press, cafes, Cheap Charlies, soapboxers, and dance
halls—was not without its own problems. Like the immigrants whom they served, these institutions were filled
with their own contradictions and paradoxes. If among the
immigrants there were con men, upwardly mobile allright-
niks, and white slave procurers, then within the *landsmanschaftn* there were petty arguments over death benefits,
within the Yiddish press there were lies and distortions,
and within the informal social settings there were mundane moments and petty problems. But on the whole this
counterworld or subculture served the immigrant remark-
ably well.

It provided him or her with a framework of familiarity and various sets of "intellectuals" who could comfort the immigrant and make sense of an otherwise bewildering world. People like Emma Goldman and Abe Cahan, Morris Hillquit and Margaret Sanger, interpreted and analyzed the complex social phenomena of life in America, and they explained each part as a facet of the whole (capitalism) which oppressed the immigrants and could be changed. Overcrowding, for example, was described as a natural outgrowth of real estate speculation. Poverty was explained as the other side of financier Jacob Schiff's wealth. And marriage—as someone like Emma Goldman saw it—was merely a slightly different form of legalized prostitution. The counterworld of the press, theater, cafes, etc., nurtured and sustained these and other schematizers of immigrant experience, these and other ideas. And it was on and through the streets of the Lower East Side of New York that these ideas took hold and were played out. The streets became a network of opposition to the way things were, and therefore an object of grave concern to the upper class, who were threatened by the radical nature of street life in the Jewish quarter.

PART ONE **The Rise of Organized Play**

*Thus saith the Lord. . . . And the streets of the city shall be
full of boys and girls playing in the streets thereof.*

—*Zechariah 8:4-5*

CHAPTER 1 **Streetwise**

The streets of the Lower East Side Jewish community were like a barrel overflowing with activities and people. Hester Street with its pushcarts and games of tag; Allen Street with its parading brothel workers and newsboys; Broome, Delancey, and the rest—all were places where several things occurred simultaneously. There was no compartmentalization into separate spaces or times. Street life was vibrant and alive with children and adults, images and fantasies. People met on the street and kibitzed or gossiped in the "jargon language of Yiddish." They went bargain hunting to the pushcarts. They formed informal "corner klatches" where the leading issues of the day were debated and discussed with a passion. Street life was where the complexities of political economy were reduced to the simple human dignity on the faces of the marching workers. Street life was where tag and one-'o-cat lived with pickle salesmen. Street life *was* life.

On the one hand, the streets, its stoops, and its corners presented the only opportunity for autonomous forms of recreation, play, and community. It was in these crevices of reality that people related to one another with their own style, in their own way, unrestricted by the factory or family. For those who wanted privacy, the streets offered anonymity; for those who wanted community, that was there too. On the other hand, the streets were more than just social settings: they were the arena for spontaneous and organized political action involving everything from soapbox orations to the protest marches of the Socialist-led unions to enraged residents attacking upper-class bicyclists who sped through the Lower East Side on the way to work.

"Wheeling to work" was quite common among the young, smartly-dressed accountants and clerks who lived uptown but worked on Wall Street. Every weekday morning they transformed the streets of the East Side south of Fourteenth Street into "natural" thoroughfares on which safety was sacrificed to speed. Indeed, hardly a morning went by without a child being run over or an elderly person knocked to the ground. One cyclist, Edwin T. Christmae of Grace and Company at Hanover Square put it this way:

> The children in the streets are so numerous that it is impossible to avoid riding them down. I have run down three children while riding through these streets, but the accident was absolutely unavoidable.[1]

The immigrants on the Lower East Side responded to the cyclists by calling upon common experiences of marauding pogromists. Many of them were only months away from attacks suffered at the hands of rampaging cossacks in Europe; they remembered and fought back. On Division Street, on Forsythe and other through streets to the financial district, catcalls and jeers greeted the "monkeys on wheels." The people of the ghetto covered the streets with glass, garbage, and sharp stones. They pelted the cyclists with eggs and vegetables and used pushcarts to block the riders' progress.

The conflict between the bicyclists and the people categorized by the *New York Times* as "ignorant and misguided foreigners"[2] became an important issue for the *Times* which gave it considerable coverage during a four-month period in 1896. "The residents of that district seem to take a malignant delight in revenging the persecutions they underwent by becoming persecutors themselves on arriving here," the paper railed as it called for "instant measures" to remedy such an abhorrent state of affairs. Eventually, police from the Eldridge Street Station were assigned to protect the riders.

The attacks on the cyclists were not simple events of hooliganism nor were they as politically significant as the immigrants' more tightly organized protests like the cloakmakers' strike of 1894[3] or the garment strikes of the next decade. In many ways, they resembled the Luddites' (English artisans of the early 1800s) response to the introduction of machinery. The Luddites smashed machines and burned factories while the Jewish immigrants pelted cyclists and obstructed traffic. Both groups were reacting to a changing way of life where the tempo, direction and conditions of the change unfolded beyond the control of the "changed." If the Luddites were artisans caught between the rise of laissez-faire and the decline of craft and community, then the Jews of the Lower East Side, a closely knit communal people, were the first victims of urban renewal and the city government's plans to make way for progress.

This road to progress was to be paved not with gold, but with asphalt. Starting in the winter of 1894, a campaign for the widespread use of asphalt was begun by the reformers and endorsed by incoming Mayor William Strong and the Board of Estimate and Apportionment. Thanks to asphalt, the lower class would be cured of poor health habits, epidemics would be staved off, quick means of transportation would be provided, ghetto dwellers' recreation opportunities would be improved, and, the cost of moving commodities would be reduced. In a lengthy article on May 30, 1895, entitled "Asphalt for the Poor," the *New York Times* extolled the remarkable qualities of asphalt streets:

> Streets have been selected for asphalt pavement that will extend the present lines of transportation and open routes across the city which will cheapen the delivery of goods and give comfortable access to some of the more important ferries....It is however as a sanitary appliance that an asphalt pavement presents the greatest value. It is nearly a non-absorbent, it is free from cracks that offer lurking places for disease germs, and can be thoroughly washed

whenever it is thought advisable....The establishment of main routes of communication between different parts of the city which connect with our parks, ferries, and railroad stations, seems to me [water Purveyor Edward P. North] but little less important than conserving the health of our poorest population.[4]

The plans for asphalting received a $3 million appropriation from the legislature and involved covering streets in the region "occupied by our wage earning class" and linking them to those already asphalted as far north as 86th Street on the East Side and 119th Street on the West Side.[5] Led by Socialist and Anarchist intellectuals, many of the immigrants opposed the plan on the grounds that it would simply make their community more vulnerable to invasion by "scorchers on wheels."[6] They argued that everyone would be in danger of being run over and that the children's play areas would become unsafe. The *Times* denounced these "demagogues of the district" for not wanting to make the conditions of the ghetto "more habitable and more human."[7] But the issue wasn't really whether or not the opponents of asphalt wanted to improve the conditions of their family or friends. As a matter of fact, the very people who opposed asphalt were often the loudest spokesmen for improvements in public health, education and working conditions. The real issue was the street—its definition and control.

On this issue, opinion varied. Jacob Riis, journalist, urban reformer, and playground advocate, saw the street as an institution that contributed to the disintegration of character and the destruction of communal bonds in the slum. He believed that it was impossible for a ghetto child to build character in the streets "because character implies depth, a soil, and growth. The street is all surface: nothing grows there; it only hides a sewer."[8] Because he saw the street as an unmitigated evil, Riis became a leading crusader for the playground movement, writing numerous articles and giving scores of lectures in favor of playgrounds and in opposition to street play.

A report of the University Settlement Society at the turn of the century saw things a little more dialectically. It recognized some positive aspects of street life and culture, but essentially agreed with Riis:

> In the summer the adults come to the front of their houses for fresh air and gossip. The doorstep becomes the local forum....Every night the main thoroughfares provide a promenade for thousands who find in walk and talk along the pavement a cheap form of social entertainment....
>
> But at the best, the social adult life in the streets is tame compared with the merry games of the children. To them the crowded thoroughfare is a relief from the more crowded room, and the games with little comrades a happy change from nursing baby and cleaning-up....
>
> But the life of the street is at best a rough school of experience and at its worst, a free field in which the most evil and corrupting influence may work against the morals of the community....[9]

To Harry Roskolenko and Samuel Chotzinoff, both of whom grew to adulthood amid the sights and smells of the Lower East Side, the streets represented drama:

> There were ambulances to be run after and horsecars to hang on to unobserved by the conductor. If one was on intimate terms with a currier in a livery stable, one could sit bareback astride a horse and ride bareback through the streets. Something was constantly happening which one had to repair to the spot to see at first hand....Fires broke out constantly in all seasons, and the air was seldom free from the clang of the fire engines, the shrieks of the siren, and the clatter of the horses on the cobblestones. Following the fire engines could conceivably occupy all one's leisure time....[10]
>
> We knew all about death as children learn about death [from accidents, fires, collapsing tenements.] The bodies would be laid out in the streets....[11]

Clara Hooper, an admirer of Emma Goldman and a garment worker while a young woman growing up on the Lower East Side, remembers the streets as labor markets:

> Those people who worked on machines in the garment industry who were called operators at that time had to carry their own machines. They would carry the head of the

machine, come out to Hester Street, sit down on the asphalt, and wait. The employer would come over; he would look at the machine first to see if the man had a good machine and then he would talk to him about hiring. But this was really an excruciating thing that the man would have to carry his own machine and if he was employed he would have to put it back on his shoulder and carry it up to the shop....We used to go to the library past there and we would see them sitting and those that were not employed would remain there on the benches—very downcast, very downhearted. The place was always crowded, mostly middle-age men as girls were spared this indignity. They were usually hired by recommendation.[12]

Morris Mikelbank, who came to America in 1911 at the age of sixteen and who lived on Pitt Street in the world of revolutionary ideals, remembers the streets as political arenas:

The entire block was filled at least in the morning hours. And this also remained a spot for those who came to preach all kinds of ideas and ideals including the Socialists. The assembly was ready made for them; all they had to do was to bring a soap-box or a stand and up they went to talk to the people. They didn't have to hire a hall. That remained until right after the first World War. I remember Debs used to come there during election time.

And other times people would come and try to organize. They told me that the employers are going to take advantage of you and try to exploit you. They should not let themselves be exploited; they should see that if they are not payed well enough they should ask for a raise, which was not an easy thing to do. But, they tried to enlighten the workers—that they had value—that they mean something [despite the fact that] the employer only wanted to pay them $3 dollars a week including the use of their machines.[13]

On different levels and with varying degrees of correctness, all the observers were right. Any street "offers a wide variety of spaces that are highly adaptable and given to both stationary and mobile use."[14] The streets of the Lower East Side were neither the Paradise Lost that Roskolenko and Chotzinoff thought them to be nor the dens of depravity assumed by Riis and the reformers. They were both—good and bad.

While it is true that on the whole street life was freer of the social maladies of capitalism than the factory or the family, the streets were not without their own problems—for both immigrants and reformers.

One problem was the youth gangs, although they were not nearly as many nor as bellicose as the reformers portrayed them. Ben Levine, a former gang member turned reporter, remembers that being in a gang meant being together in "a loose sort of group," playing together and occasionally defending your turf or hoping to pass safely through the territory of another gang. "What streeter?" was the universally acknowledged warning-cum-greeting that could lead to a beating if your street was currently held in disfavor. But "It wasn't very sinister or very strong. Some of them grew into gangs out of which came gangsters, but not many."[15] Chotzinoff writes that "The law [also] frowned on gangs. For that reason it behooved one to belong to a gang." There were rival gangs that issued ultimatums to one another and battled with sticks and stones. Yet things were not so serious as to withstand the call of relatives and "interruptions at dinnertime."[16]

Political and labor battles involving anarchists, socialists, the politically conservative Orthodox, and Tammany Hall were another problem. Tammany goons frequently created disturbances at Socialist soapbox rallies, and Tammany-controlled police were hardly impartial to labor's efforts to organize. In October of 1894, for example, a gathering of some 3,500 people assembled at Rutgers Square in support of the cloakmakers' strike. Before the scheduled march could take place, the crowd was ordered to disperse by the police. When they refused, the protesters were attacked by the officers wielding clubs and firing their revolvers into the air. An investigation of this "police riot," as it was characterized by an attorney for the strikers, concluded that "some force had to be used." As the official investigator saw it, the rights of free speech and assembly were less important than the problems that arose when "the square was blocked and traffic was impeded."[17]

More troublesome than street demonstrations to social reformers were the pushcarts that dotted the Lower East Side. For people like Eddie Cantor and his family, pushcarts were responsible for filling the air with the delicious scents of cheese (the carts on Orchard Street), herring (the pushcarts of Hester Street), and all the good things of life. But uninitiated uptowners and reformers, who believed that air was "tasteless, odorless [and] colorless"[18] campaigned vigorously against what they called the pushcart menace. Reform Streets Commissioner George Waring said, "The Hester Street market has been an illegal nuisance to the community," and claimed that pushcarts were an affront to the "respectable merchants who pay taxes and rent."[19] The *New York Times* and many shopkeepers joined the commissioner in this refrain, the *Times* even going so far as to claim in an editorial that an irresponsible member of the community like the pushcart peddler raised "children that don't learn good citizenship," becoming instead "street arabs." For the clinching blow in a drive to get rid of the carts, some of America's wealthiest men described the peddlers and their obstructionist vehicles as "agents of a trust"—an accusation hard to reconcile with the eight to ten cents a day rental fees for pushcarts.[20]

If the streets were full of their own contradictions, including gangs and pushcarts, political battles and fights for territory, nowhere was there a more complex problem than in the area of sex. Psychologists, settlement house workers, playground directors, feminists, parents, and children all were concerned about "The Sex Question." Everyone felt that in one way or another the question of sex was connected to the street as problem or possibility. Some felt the streets were tracks of temptation; others saw them as avenues of escape from the stultification of the family; still others saw streets as sex information centers:

> A most serious evil in the street life of the older boys and girls is their behavior toward one another...in the streets and hallways which provide conditions which at least make for absolute vulgarity and have destroyed many a boy's or girl's character.[21]

Thus cautioned the University Settlement in its "Annual

Report" of 1900. The leading psychologist of the period, G. Stanley Hall, wrote that

> Sex tension is one of the subtle and most potent of all psychological agencies. Each ought to find the presence of the other the tonic and stimulus to its very highest and best achievements, but incessant and prolonged familiarity [such as continued street contact] wears down this idealizing influence to the dull monotony of the daily routine.[22]

Harry Roskolenko remembers the street as the place where you learned "about sex" but in a way somewhat different from that perceived or understood by the settlement workers and psychologists. He recalls: "They would, too, nurse their babies in front of our eyes by merely pulling out the left or right breast, a nipple to the fore, and into some small mouth it went."[23]

Then there was Allen Street which stood for prostitution, and "white slavery" which was a common fear. Yet small boys at play with the "fallen" were a common sight, and it is not unreasonable to surmise that quite a few youngsters learned some sex physiology and prophylactic methods from such liaisons. Finally, as the first decade of the new century drew to a close, courageous women like Emma Goldman and Margaret Sanger took to the streets, soapboxes in hand, and dispensed information about birth control that alternately shocked and educated. The Orthodox, of course, denounced Goldman and Sanger from *shul* to *shul*, but thousands of people came and listened anyway—usually leaving with a little more knowledge than they had come with.

It was this incredible mix of sexuality, sarcasm, and struggle that made street culture a valuable resource for the green (brand-new immigrant) and the recently green. Irving Howe recalls:

> The streets taught us the deceits of commerce, introduced us to the excitement of sex, schooled us in strategies of survival, and gave us our first clear idea of what life in America was really going to be like.[24]

Life in America was going to require adaptability, hard work, a sense of humor, and the mutual aid of community.

If the Jewish immigrants were to realize a sense of self and assistance even as they were roughened by the actuality of bared breasts, pugnacious police, cacophonous crowds, and much more, they needed some kind of social mucilage.

A great deal of that cohesiveness was provided by street games. Children and youth bound together as teammates, competitors, and adventure seekers overlooked each other's inadequacies and looked to each other for information. When a batter broke a window with a sharply lined foul ball, they were all united in their flight from the enraged shopkeeper. When the police started their periodic crackdowns on craps, bonfires, or playing ball in the street, all the "delinquents" joined together. The solidarity that grew out of these common pursuits and predicaments helped build among the immigrants a camaraderie which would serve them well in later years as they strove to build trade unions.

Although tens of millions of people did not spend six hours of uninterrupted voyeurism as they do now on Sundays during football season, a considerable number of friends, relatives, and neighbors came out into the street to observe the children and youth at play. Their numbers were significant (and irksome to the reformers) as a recreation survey sponsored by the People's Institute in 1913 reveals:

> One of the great elements of danger lay in the fact that in the vicinity of playing youngsters the census takers counted 30,427 grown-up loungers.[25]

The study was undertaken between the hours of four and five on Saturday afternoon, April 29, and it tabulated the activities of 120,000 East Side children on the streets at that time. In addition to criticizing and fretting over the children's habits, the surveyors found time to deplore the spectating adults whom they described as "leering loungers." The study did not recognize the personal (familial, comradely) interest in the games which drew the loungers, nor did it acknowledge the freedom and joyfulness which play evokes even in those who watch and perhaps reminisce. Whatever the reason for the adults' presence, the important thing is that there *was* a presence.

This presence meant two things. First, the streets were populated and therefore safe; there was some pickpocketing and filching of fruit by the young boys, but the streets were essentially crime-free, comfortable places. Charles Stein, who was raised in the East Side neighborhood, recalls:

> There were lots of people in the streets. Where I lived, East Broadway, Grand Street, Clinton Street, all the streets were filled with foreign immigrants....
> There was no fear of holdups. We were safe.[26]

Second, there was on hand a ready crowd that could be mobilized to support strikes and join in street parades or outpourings of sympathy. During the cloakmakers' strike in 1894, for example, the whole neighborhood around the garment shops "sounded with applause from the sympathizers with the strikers."[27] When 12,000 coatmakers struck in 1907, "the streets surrounding the shop district were beleaguered by crowds."[28] And during the garment makers' strike of 1910, the entire community was transformed:

> By half past two, all the streets from 38th Street down and from the East River towards the west, were jammed with workers. In many of the streets, cars and trucks had to be stopped because of the crowds....As soon as it became known that a settlement had been reached, thousands of workers, cloakmakers and others began to gather in the streets leading to the Square where the Forward Building is located. By 7:00 o'clock, the Square and the nearby streets were jammed with people.[29]

The street games, which brought thousands of people into close contact with one another in a framework of fun and relaxation, contributed to the creation of a community. A pattern of daily recurrence developed which facilitated talking and sharing. Support for marching strikers seemed "natural." In such a community there were always eyes trained on the street[30]—mothers watching out for young ones, older brothers and sisters eyeing the skills of a younger sibling, people amused by the "serious nonseriousness" of play. This familiarity of shared experience softened feelings of anomie and rootlessness generated by immigration and constant moving. It complemented the exploitive conditions of the shop and created a framework within which the immigrants shared sorrow and gladness, serious issue and trivial details. Lunch breaks provided opportunities to gripe and organize. Likewise, evenings and days off spent on the stoops watching the kids play meant a chance to laugh and socialize. The more frequently people saw each other "on the street" the greater the likelihood a friendship would be born, a comradeship would be anchored. Playing or watching created a sense of rootedness or recurrence, and legitimized a person in the eyes of another.

The wealthy and the reformers recognized the importance of street games to the immigrants' way of life and considered both odious and dangerous. Teddy Roosevelt, quoted in the very first issue of *The Playground*, the national organized-play journal, said, "We must provide some other place than the streets for their [children's] leisure time. If we would have our citizens content and law-abiding we must not sow the seeds of discontent in childhood by denying children their birthright of play [in playgrounds]."[31] The following year, Dr. Woods Hutchinson noted at the Second Annual Recreation Congress that the streets are "as suitable for play as the track of a trunk line railway."[32] And at that same congress another leader of the organized-play movement, Arthur Leland, asked, "Have you ever driven a timorous horse on city streets during the hours when the savage hoards are no longer cooped up in the schoolroom?"[33]

The leaders of the organized-play movement devoted a great deal of time and effort to attempts to solve the street play problem. In 1905, Luther Gulick went so far as to recommend the construction of a twenty-story skyscraper for children—each floor of which would be a playground! In the second issue of *The Playground* an article entitled "A Suggestion to the Millionaire" urged that some endowed person build a series of playgrounds and summer camps to "get one million New York children off the streets." These suggestions, the article stated, are "easily within the endowment of any millionaire who loves children and the city of New York."[34] As we shall see later, the establishment of such play centers and the eradication of street play depended on more than just the beneficence of a millionaire with spare cash. Rather, the rise of organized play and the destruction of immigrant street culture was the result of the combined efforts of many of America's leading reformers operating with and on behalf of the upper class. Many tactics were used to attain their goals, including the passage of "street laws" which prohibited playing in the street, flying kites, and the like. These laws were responsible for hauling thousands of boys and girls before the children's courts from 1902 onward. In one year alone, 1909, in New York City, it was found that

> practically one half (5,733) of the total 11,494 children were taken into custody because of trivial violations, generally known as disorderly conduct. Embraced within these provisions came offenses no more serious than the playing of ball in the street, building of bon-fires, the playing of shinny and other acts growing out of the child's normal instinct for play.[35]

In addition to passing street laws, the elite and the reformers opened playgrounds and recreation piers as a way of removing the child from the street.

All of the leading private and public recreation groups took as an article of faith the need to eliminate street play and games. They saw in the "alternative attractions" of gyms, leagues, vacation schools, etc. not only lures away from the street but opportunities for socializing the newcomers to a particular value and behavior system. The children of immigrants were caught between destruction (of their street play) and construction (of class-bred alternatives). Street play and playgrounds were the two sides of the coin during this period and the children were forced to "choose sides" between them.

The reformers were interested not only in the form of recreation engaged in by the children and youth of the city, they were also interested in the content. They opposed gambling, saloons, and vaudeville and they tried to license bowling alleys and pool halls. Playground directors were instructed to familiarize themselves with and combat the existing commercial recreation establishments in their community, as the Playground Association of America campaigned against all forms of recreation that involved spending money and remaining passive. PAA president Joseph Lee himself criticized America's "half hypnotic interest in prize fights" and the "hysteria of our big football games."[36] This reform opposition to commercial recreation was based on the idea that play, recreation, and sport should be antidotes to the monotony and alienation of factory life. Leisure was seen as a trade-off, as a conscripted sphere of freedom and action outside the framework of the marketplace. The worker and his family, they believed, should be free of the rule of money in those hours when the purpose was to "recreate." The reformers wanted leisure to "bring a complete forgetfulness of other things and a loss of self-consciousness through complete absorption in the game."[37] This unconsciousness could not be attained, they presumed, if people had to pay for their leisure. Paying might carry with it a reminder of the world of work (since work was the source of the money used to play) and such a reminder might bring with it feelings of anger or despair caused by dissatisfaction with wages or the wage system. Well financed campaigns against commercial recreation resulted from these fears of the reformers whose final word was that money and recreation should not mix.

But many of the non-commercial recreations that filled the gutters of Division, Essex, and Hester Street were also denounced by reformers and the upper class. In 1905, for example, John Chase, headworker at the Maxwell House Settlement, conducted a walking tour of the Lower East Side and noted that playing with fire and "craps" were the two most popular games, followed by marbles, potsie, leapfrog, jumping rope, baseball, cat, buttons, and tops. He concluded that "The gambling instinct is very strong...the fire instinct is very strong...and the running games...are replaced by cramped games such as leapfrog, hopskotch, etc."[38] A 1910 survey conducted by the New York Parks and Playground Association made similar findings and observed how the street games of immigrant children were a menace to the municipality (bonfires, for example, were said to have caused $25,000 worth of damage).[39]

Both the Chase survey and that by the Parks and Playgrounds received wide dissemination in the settlement, charity, and popular press. They were part of a vast propaganda campaign aimed at arousing the public in support of municipally funded and operated play facilities. Although their methodologies were highly questionable (no cross-checks, small population samples not randomly selected, etc.), these researches into the play life of immigrant children were the first of their kind and they won legitimacy almost by default. In 1913, the People's Institute conducted an even more elaborate, if still scientifically crude, investigation. Over 500 settlement, church, and social workers from 38 organizations checklisted all the activities of 120,000 children, cataloguing some 52 different types of games. The activities were distributed as follows:[40]

Idling	27,604
Watching others play	23,971
Unclassified	23,406
Wholesale competitive games	20,341
Baseball	13,069
Caring for babies	4,711
Constructive play	1,168
Team games	808
Gambling	749
Bonfires	143

What do these studies tell us? What can we conclude? First, we note that less than 13 percent of all children were engaged in team games. At a time when capitalism was moving from its anarchic, entrepreneurial stage to one in which cooperation (trusts) ruled, this low percentage of team play could be seen as a problem. How would a young worker learn how to fit himself into an increasingly group-oriented industrial process as a member of an assembly line or as a representative of the corporation if he did not learn teamwork in the games of his youth?

Second, we see from these statistics that more children were idling and watching than were involved in competitive games. For a country that prided itself on the active participation of its citizenry, for a country which prided itself on being a democracy compared to European autocracies and monarchies, the idleness of the children could only be considered unhealthy. The reformers feared that if immigrants did not participate in games when they were young, they would not know how to participate *correctly* when they got older. Having forfeited an early opportunity to learn self-control and proper conduct they would be candidates for mob action and anarchy. Spectatorism, in the view of organized-play leaders, was a dangerous thing.

Finally, we observe that almost as many children were gambling as were playing team games, except for baseball. These children would never learn that hard work, not luck, was the stuff of success. Despite tales of Horatio Alger and living success stories of people like Andrew Carnegie, these immigrant youth put more faith in the roll of the dice than in the rewards of the system. It was feared that such an attitude, while limited to a small number at the time of the survey, could spread and weaken America's resolve.

All of the statistics and implications of the People's Institute study merely "proved" what had been obvious to the upper class and reformers since 1894—that immigrant youth needed supervision, energizing, organization, and moral uplift. If the immigrants would realize the folly of their and their children's way, they could be led to a better life where boys became men, girls their feminine counterparts, and most importantly, they all became more efficient and less class-conscious workers helping to make America great.

But as we have seen in their ideas about streets, protests, and culture, the Jewish immigrants of the Lower East Side had their own definitions of reality, their own values and goals. It would be no easy task for the upper class to root its world view in the culture of these workers and their children. The wealthy controlled the factories and the economy, the elections and the courts, the schools and the systems of charity, but the street life of the immigrants was beyond their command. It was a pleasant counterworld that provided a respite from the oppressive nature of social relations shaped exclusively by money, power, and profit. Built on patterns deeply buried in the culture of Eastern Europe, built on poverty and hope, such a tradition did not die easily. In fact, reform efforts to Americanize these immigrants by breaking up this "alien" culture lasted from 1894 to 1914. During that time the reformers and the immigrants were locked in a struggle in the streets and the shops, in the parks and on the playgrounds, over the control of street life, the rise of organized play, and the "problem" of leisure.

Play to order is no longer play; it could at best be a forcible imitation of it.

—Johan Huizinga

CHAPTER 2 **The Leisure-Time Problem**

When the New Industrial Era emerged after the Civil War, some members of the upper class realized that the types and amounts of recreation available to the poor were inadequate and inappropriate. The game of life that had evolved from urbanization, rapid industrialization, and immigration was quicker and more complex. Work was more intense and required more training and discipline, but there were also more opportunities for leisure. The length of the working day, through a combination of technological and working-class political advances, was being shortened. The need to educate vast numbers of people, to make them literate and functional in a symbol- and word-filled world, was extending childhood. And the huge influx of immigrants created "labor surpluses" when capital contracted, and thus unemployment also increased. All these developments—the shorter work day, longer childhoods, greater unemployment—spelled an increase in time available for leisure. People like iron magnate Abraham Hewitt, nurse-reformer Lilian Wald, child-study psychologist G. Stanley Hall, Joseph Lee, and others, recognized that life in the postwar era was, in a sense, a whole new ballgame, in which leisure would play a critically important position. They set out to construct a theory and build a movement that could incorporate leisure into the structure and value system of capitalism.

But while the organized-play people concentrated on the working class, that class all but ignored the rise of organized play. Preoccupied with the demands of work which meant twelve, fourteen, and sometimes sixteen hours a day in the shop, the workers had never devoted much of their attention or resources to the active pursuit of leisure. Play, especially for the immigrants, was an accepted part of the rhythms of life, not an object of study and design. Recreation was that which could be offered by the various immigrant and working-class clubs, lodges, and neighborhood entrepreneurs. A glimpse of the life and thoughts of Isidore Kanowitz, a ninety-one-year-old, life-long resident of the Lower East Side, reveals the immigrants' limited understanding of the importance of play.

The son of a cap and hat operator, brother of six boys and two girls, Izzy left school early and found his way around the neighborhood with his fists and feet. He could punch "and take a punch"; he could sprint away from the sound of onrushing cops coming to bust up a craps game. He jostled for space on the corner of Allen Street to sell his newspapers and make some money for his family and himself. But although wise in the ways of jabs and jobs, his perception of the significance of his life and particularly of his street play is too modest:

> It didn't mean nothin' playin' baseball in those days. We used to get a five-cent bat and a two-cent ball and play barehanded in the middle of the street. Sometimes we'd get chased by a storekeeper who was afraid we'd break a window. Some of them thought they owned the street. But it didn't mean nothin'.[1]

His characterization of street play as meaningless is typical of the attitude of most of the immigrants of the period. What they worried about was work, not play. What they "practiced" was labor militancy, not culture consciousness.

Meanwhile, the reformers were taking play very seriously. Listen to the Boston Brahmin Joseph Lee, who became one of the country's foremost authorities on play:

> Play is the intensest part of the life of a child, and it is therefore in his play hours that his most abiding lessons are learned, that his most central and determining growth takes place.[2] Play is to the boy what work is to the man—the fullest attainable expression of what he is and the effective means of becoming more.[3]

Lee and his fellow advocates of organized play were right. But they had the wrong reasons.

Play is important because it links the past with the present and the future, because it connects the body with its background, because it helps the child understand relationships of time, space, and motion. It is an art form, a mode of physical expression, and a restatement or a transcendence of the social order.[4] It can point toward an entirely new definition of the status quo and thus threaten the status quo.[5] Because of this threat it invites colonization through cooptation, compartmentalization, and centralization. The result is a social form known as "hegemony."[6]

Hegemony is a process wherein the values and goals of one class become the generally accepted values and goals of the whole society. In a colonial society where the settler class controls the tempo of social life, hegemony manifests itself as natives begin to take on the attitudes and appearances of the colonists. This mimicry extends to religion, dress, recreation—in fact, to almost every aspect of the natives' lives. In a class society such as the United States, we find the lower or working classes mirroring the styles and social norms of their betters. Our folk language captures the essence of hegemony when we think of "passing for white" or "acting like gold so as to be treated like silver." When Afro-Americans straighten their hair, when Jewish-Americans straighten their noses, and when immigrants "Americanize" (change) their surnames—hegemony lives. In sum, hegemony is the "spontaneous" consent given by the majority (the working class regardless of ethnicity) to the general direction imposed on social life by the ruling minority, and it derives from the position and power of that class.

The first stage of developing hegemonic control requires

a redefinition of the status quo in line with the dominant group's perception. Everything which is not a part of the structure of the Establishment is made to appear dangerous or impossible.[7] At the turn of the century, for example, the Jewish immigrant's street culture, reflecting as it did the folkways of a people caught in the pressures of industrialization, was a lively, free-form escape from the onus of coordinated time, compartmentalized space, and rigid social relationships. It was an opportunity for children to evolve their own forms of organization, to honor their own imagination, and to explore the social terrain of the community. Adults likewise fashioned their own social networks and controlled the pace and space of communal life. The upper class saw this autonomy of people who, "acted like savages"[8] as clearly hostile and dangerous. They condemned the "Saturday night debauches and Sunday carnivals" because "he who indulges in them will in time become a striker for higher wages."[9] And they wanted each immigrant to receive athletic training so that "he will neither shrink from imaginary danger nor shirk manual work which falls to his lot."[10]

In order to extend their control of the immigrants beyond the door of the factory and beyond the length of the workday, it was necessary for the upper class to shape time, space, and motion. By organizing the work week, holidays, time off, overtime, and leisure time as they saw fit, the powerful could solidify their control over the social process. By organizing and shaping space—public space, parks, streets, tenements, etc.—the wealthy and the reformers could contain any movement away from capitalism. And by controlling motion—rapid transit, bicycles, movement to the outer boroughs, etc.—they could regulate and thus control the tempo of the immigrant masses. Time, space, and motion are elements common to both labor and leisure. By controlling time and space in one sphere—either in work, or in play—one class is more likely to gain control over another. The greater control that one class has over time and space, the greater control it can have over another class.

This control or hegemony does not spring up overnight.

The struggle for hegemony and the subsets of time, space, and motion *is* a struggle. It is a struggle marked by consolidation and compromise, filled with machination and design, and determined by some events that are planned and others that are not. In the main, hegemony works to subvert those parts of the workers' culture that are weakest and most malleable. In 1911, Howard Braucher, secretary of the Playground Association of America, articulated this principle which had been initiated by the first settlement workers:

> It is felt that few institutions in America have such an opportunity to influence the development of neighborhood character as has the play center. In leisure time, men and women give best expression of what they really are; in leisure time, men and women are MOST EASILY INFLU-ENCED: the songs which are sung in the play centers, the idealism which permeates the atmosphere, the spirit of the athletic contests and games, enters the soul of those who come day after day, and night after night to the play centers.[11]

"Entering the soul" of the workers was exactly what the reformers had in mind, according to historian Roy Lubove:

> Members of the privileged classes would live with the poor as friends and neighbors, interpreting their needs and aspirations to the community while introducing into the life of the poor the spiritual and cultural advantages which poverty had denied them.[12]

The schematization of experience, the interpretation of reality, and the imposition of standards by fashioning images of "the good" were all facets of the drive toward hegemony. But the function and outcome of this schematization was quite unusual. The reformers thought they could simply impose their definitions on the children, while the youth, in machine-like fashion, would process the data and reorient their values and ideals accordingly. Such a lock-step interpretation of the assimilation of definitions had its roots in the Lancasterian system of education propounded for the public schools. Here, information was disseminated and absorbed, with regurgitation serving as confirmation of the system's effectiveness. Affect was irrelevant.[13] But when the same approach was taken with play, what resulted was fantasy rather than fact. The world and world view of people like PAA president Joseph Lee struck the immigrant child as so odd or unreal that the youngsters saw it as alluring and/or nonthreatening.[14] Eddie Cantor, who called himself "a typical New York street boy," remembers his first visit at the age of eleven, early on in the century, to the reformers' world of the Educational Alliance's Cold Springs Camp. His description confirms historian Allen Davis's claim that "there was an element of the unreal and esoteric about the early settlement workers' attempts to dispense the culture of the universities to working-men."[15] Cantor recalls:

> Cold Springs was a strange place. There wasn't a horsecar or a deli store in it...[instead there were] endless playgrounds. [It was] a strange, magic world with fruits on trees instead of pushcarts.

The physical mysteriousness had its "theoretical" counterpart, as Eddie discovered after being caught stealing two blankets by the camp's director:

> "I know you feel chilly at night and like to keep warm, but when you steal two blankets from the other cots that means that two other little boys lie all night without blankets and feel very cold. Now is that right?" Eddie felt embarrassed: "I had never been reprimanded quite so gently....Instead of a scowl I got a smile; instead of a blow, a pat on the cheek. Yes, life was totally different in this marvelous boys' heaven...."

Of course, the effect of this process, though powerful, is not and was not as swift in the accomplishment of salvation as the reformers would have wished. Cantor noted the antisocial impact of his actions, but was not completely overwhelmed: "The next night I stole only one blanket."[16]

The point should not be lost in the humor of the example. The working class has its own image of the future ensconced as fantasy. Hegemony involves the subversion of the fantasy process and the simultaneous imposition of an image of the possible manufactured by the dominant class. This image is an idealization of existing reality (in the case of Cantor and the camp it was social harmony). But because the image of possibility put forward by the powerful emerges from capitalism, a social structure built on contradiction, the ideal is unattainable. (In the case of Cantor, scarcity amid plenty was the problem.) Working-class efforts to accomplish the ideal result in the transformation of the subject, not the object; thus, what transpires is restatement and alienation, not transcendence or transformation.

Not surprisingly, this process of cultural imperialism and the realization of hegemony took many forms, in line with Reich's assertion that "class consciousness is to be found in every nook and cranny of everyday life."[17] In some instances it was an innocent process of the reformers' unconsciously imposing their world view and background assumptions on the workers/immigrants. In the manner in which they talked, the carriage they held, the informal topics of discussion they engaged in, and in countless other interactions of exposures, they conveyed a value judgment. In other instances, however, the process of cultural imperialism was much more blatant and involved an actual calculation of intent based on a class-logical assessment of the situation. Witness the words of James B. Reynolds, headworker at the University Settlement in 1900:

> We have in fact before us a question of COLONIAL ADMINISTRATION, the colony having established itself with us instead of being established by us.[18]

Excepting the fact that the colony was really "the colonies" and that the question of the dynamics of immigration is more problematic than Reynolds asserts (some of the colonies having been established at least partially as a result of the thrust of U.S. foreign policy and a mixture of imperial politics and imperial financing), the intent of such a statement is clear. Since, as Lukacs points out, the bourgeoisie has the advantage over the proletariat organizationally and intellectually, while the proletariat's advantage lies in its ability to see the whole and thus act in such a way as to change reality, that ability must be blunted.[19] The proletariat's perception of the totality of a capitalist social system derives from its position in the productive process and allows it to see and act on the potential for change. Its perception informs the nature of its action as it struggles to liberate itself, and in so doing abolish class society as such. Hence, the need for organizing the everyday life of the working class by integrating it with the bourgeois order, albeit as an inferior partner, a sort of "farm club" for the major (bourgeois) leagues. The elite were not out to destroy the immigrants; they merely wanted to integrate, regulate, and relegate them to an inferior status.

The move toward integration demanded the establishment of "alternative attractions" which would capture the attention and win the allegiance of the working class. These attractions included roof gardens, outings, boat rides, lectures, sports leagues, domestic science classes, and much more. They will be the topics of further investigation throughout this book. The techniques of coercion and allurement that the reformers used will be described. But for now it is important to consider that the move to establish "alternative attractions" implied the existence of cultural norms within the immigrant "colony" that the organized-play proponents tried to supplant. This process of supplanting is the history of play in the Progressive Era in the United States—a period of consolidation and control which parallels similar developments in the body politic.

The consolidation of capital demanded a centralization of the everyday life of its subjects. In the United States, massive corporate consolidation followed the passage of the Sherman Antitrust Act in 1890. From 1897 through 1904, corporations with assets totalling $6 billion were organized, compared with $1 billion from 1879 to 1897. By 1904, monopoly capital was a reality as the top 4 percent of American concerns produced 57 percent of the total industrial output and value.[20] At the turn of the century, New York City was the center of this financial and industrial whirlwind as 69 of the 185 largest industrial combinations in the country had their head offices there.

The port facilities handled nearly two-thirds of the nation's imports, by value, and shipped abroad approximately 40 percent the total exports.[21] With this increase of wealth at one pole came, as Marx had predicted, a corresponding decrease of wealth at the other. The working class suffered 35,000 on-the-job deaths and over half a million injuries per year from 1888 to 1908 as capital sped up and thereby ground down its workers. In the realm of culture, capitalist hegemony was ascending with the same force and with a corresponding effect on the hearts and minds of the people that industrial "growth" was having on their bodies.

Capitalism was moving toward the construction of a smooth-functioning social unit built on hierarchy, fragmentation, and free choice within conscripted spheres. It was moving toward the integration of the working class within capitalist ideological norms. Simultaneously, it was moving to destroy or disintegrate those vestiges of working-class culture, like street play, that it perceived as threatening.

Integration and disintegration—both were necessary elements in the destruction of immigrant life and the building of mass culture. The New York City "Report on the Vacation Schools and Playgrounds of 1900" pointed this out as it described the failures and successes of playgrounds. It noted that the playgrounds, started by the Board of Education in 1895 as a result of the agitation of Jacob Riis and the 1894 Tenement House Commission's successful lobbying for a compulsory school playground law, were initially unsuccessful. The law had provided that every new school building was to have an attached playground organized and operated by the Board of Education, and in five years, by 1900, there were over fifty such playgrounds. But their acceptance by the youth of the neighborhood (almost all were on the Lower East Side) hinged on more than the mere provision of swings and sandboxes. Acceptance was achieved only after the delegation of

> minor responsibilities to the older boys, the most troublesome group....Once some activities were supervised by the boys, other children had eagerly volunteered their services. Very quickly...leaders and groups were formed;

specific work was arranged; a time was set for everything;
and a place and duty for every person.[22]

Thus, not until the rebellious (or the class-conscious, if you
will) were integrated into the framework of power and
authority could the ruling class's sense of time, definition
of space, and interpretation of social relations be secured
and the immigrants' patterns be broken.

At the heart of the effort of colonization was the child.
As historian Robert Wiebe points out, the central theme of
humanitarian progressivism was the child: "He united the
campaign for health, education and a richer city environment and he dominated much of the interest in labor
legislation. The child was the carrier of tomorrow's hope
whose innocence and freedom made him singularly recep-
tive to education in rational, human behavior."[23] At the
heart of the child was play. The 1898 report of the
University Settlement recognized the connection:

> Waterloo was won in part on the playing fields of Eton said
> Wellington; good government for New York may partially
> be won on the playgrounds of the East Side.[24]

Jacob Riis was inclined to speak a bit more bluntly:

> The problem of the children is the problem of the State. As
> we mould the children of the toiling masses in our cities, so
> we shape the destiny of the State....[25]

The analysis having been rendered, what remained was to
formulate policy, secure its implementation, and create a
climate for the program's acceptance. This could be done
by simultaneously defaming and destroying immigrant and
working-class culture and idealizing the reformers' alternatives—settlements, domestic science classes, and playgrounds.

From the day of his birth, the individual is made to feel that there is only one way of getting along in this world—by echoing, repeating, imitating his surroundings, by adapting himself to all the powerful things to which he eventually belongs by transforming himself from a human being into a member of organizations.

—Max Horkheimer

CHAPTER 3 **Settlements,
Schools, and Playgrounds**

Jacob Riis thought the problem of the children was the problem of the state, and Charles McCarthy, director of research for the U.S. Commission on Industrial Relations, agreed:

> The backbone is that the state must invest in human beings in the same way as you invest in cattle on a farm . . . You have got to have better human beings.

> [When asked if his idea was to build up people physically, he replied:] Yes, using the word "physical" in a big sense; physically, mentally and all those things. A man will produce more, and the employer will get more for his money, and the state will get more out of the man, and my idea is that the state ought to invest in the health, strength, intelligence and ability of the people who make up the state.[1]

These words were spoken in 1912. By then government or the state had begun a vast program of organized recreation on the municipal level; city governments across the nation were building parks, forming recreation commissions, and hiring play leaders. Twenty years earlier, when Jacob Riis spoke of the problem of children, there were no public bridges between youth and play. The organized-play programs that existed were privately funded and operated by settlement houses, charity organizations, and civic reformers. However, the tempo of industrial America quickened and the number of immigrants grew so large that private efforts to organize play were overwhelmed by the magnitude of the undertaking. The organized-play leaders, recognizing their limitations, called on the state to assume the burden of recreation for the masses.

This goal required a dual strategy: a rationale had to be developed; and simultaneously, government apparatuses had to be improved to accommodate new functions. In the first instance, the concepts of laissez-faire and Darwin's "survival of the fittest" had to be replaced with the idea of a responsive and responsible social order. In the second, private play organizations—the settlements, the Outdoor Recreation League, et al.—had to conceive, initiate, and run sample programs which would be taken over by the government if they were successful. They had to act as the research and development arms of the organized play movement, transferring information, personnel, and programs to city, state, and federal institutions. With this transfer of functions, which I shall call the "municipalization of leisure," came calculation and standardization. The government if they were successful. They had to act as the research and development arms of the organized-play movement, transferring information, personnel, and pro- yet to recover.

The first step taken toward developing an organization and strategy to define and control the play of the poor and working classes actually began with a campaign against certain ideas that existed within the upper class. While some members of the upper class like Joseph Lee, John D. Rockefeller, Jacob Schiff, and Felix Warburg understood the necessity of viewing parks as potential play sites and supported the development of organized play, others did not. Thus, before the organized-play movement could get started in its drive for government support, it had to challenge the outdated beliefs and attitudes held by members of its own class. This challenge began with an attack on the romantic landscape architecture associated with Frederick Law Olmsted.

Olmsted's style, imposed on park space across the land, was uniquely appropriate to the world view of an elite whose sense of time had a leisurely pace to it. The upper crust strolled, called on one another, sipped tea, and generally approached the environment with an almost timeless sedateness. Landscape architecture, which held a park to be more demure than vibrant, spectatorial as opposed to participatory, fitted this sensibility perfectly. In the post–Civil War period up on through the early 1890s, "The chief active uses of Central Park were the horseback riding and carriage driving of the rich,"[2] according to recreation historian Richard Knapp. "KEEP OFF THE GRASS" signs abounded, and the only way one could indulge a passion even for baseball was to secure a permit from the Parks Department. The thoughts of landscape gardener N. Janssen Rose on the reconstruction of Seward Park in the early 1900s are a good example of the elite's perception of parks and their use:

> It now remained to be considered how much of the park area should be set aside for playgrounds and how much for general park purposes. It was found upon investigation that the Neighborhood for miles around the park is crowded with hard-working people, who during their day's work have no lack of healthful exercise and who during their leisure hours would be more inclined to quiet rest, such as a park under ordinary conditions would afford.[3]

Contrarily, the reformers thought that a park should primarily be designed and equipped to accommodate active recreation—sports, gymnastics, games, and the like.[4] Toward that goal they concentrated on liberalizing park rules, freeing funds for playgrounds and small parks which had been appropriated by the legislature but which remained unspent, and on getting a representative appointed to the Park Board.

By 1910, with the appointment of Charles Stover of the Metropolitan Parks Association as parks commissioner, all these goals had been achieved. The struggle between these two different sectors of the upper class had ended with a total victory for the reformers; henceforth, all their energies could be concentrated on the working class.

The rise of organized play began in New York City in 1890 with the founding of the New York Society for Parks and Playgrounds for Children. The general impetus for the organization derived from New York City's status as a haven for immigrants and therefore as a center for Socialism, anarchism, militant trade unionism, and other "foreign" philosophies. Organizing the play of the immigrants' children was seen as part of a concerted effort to counter the intergenerational influence of such dangerous ideas. But if the general impetus for the establishment of the Society for Parks and Playgrounds came from an elite concern about potential lawlessness, the immediate impetus for the society came from within the law itself. A bill passed in 1888 allowed fifteen or more adults to establish a corporation to provide parks and playgrounds, and Charles Stover, Abraham Hewitt, and journalist Walter Vrooman did just that. According to Vrooman, the purpose of their society was to:

> furnish eventually, for all boys and girls, at public expense, the playgrounds which not even the wealthy parents now provide for their children....invoke immediately private liberality in furnishing temporary playgrounds which shall be models for municipal imitation...obtain the cooperation of the labor unions and political organizations.[5]

The first effort made on behalf of model playgrounds by the society was moderately successful. Although they were only able to raise slightly over $2,000 for their projects in more than two years of fundraising, it was enough to open a model playground in 1891 at a startup cost of $200 and $5-a-day operating expenses.[6] The law said that a private playground organization "could establish its own rules and private police force to keep order on its property, and the New York Society for Parks and Playgrounds did so.[7] "The children are controlled by an employee of the Society, who...has police powers over them while on or near the playground" read a report on the playground which stood on Second Avenue at 91st Street.[8]

This particular playground died an early death, as might be expected since a theory of and strategy for play in urban America had not yet been developed. These nascent play organizers were leaders of the national Progressive movement which, according to Richard Hofstadter, "at its heart was an effort to realize familiar and traditional ideals under novel circumstances."[9] The novel circumstances could be traced to the effects of capital's extending its institutional structures for reproducing and expanding itself through merger, concentration, and monopoly. Urbanization intensified, and immigration, the source of the cheap labor required for the expansion of capital, grew. Cities like New York were forced to incorporate surrounding areas to accommodate the rapidly increasing population, and still there was intense overcrowding in the poor and working-class neighborhoods like the Lower East Side.

At the same time that they were the causes and beneficiaries of this stage of capital accumulation, people like Abraham Hewitt, Columbia University president Seth Low, Charles Stover, and financier DeWitt Seligman (all of whom were on the Board of Trustees of the New York Society) were also victims of the process. The polychromic environment of New York City, whose pace quickened and whose boundaries were aburst with the arrival of expropriated farmers and "dark and dangerous" immigrants, jarred them. They sought refuge in organizations like the society and the settlement houses, which were intended to uplift the immigrants and habitualize them to the new American Way of Life.

The Educational Alliance

From 1893 onward, every day of the year (holidays included), the doors to the Educational Alliance building on the corner of Jefferson Street and East Broadway swung open, and thousands upon thousands of immigrants entered.[10] In the mornings, the hallways rang with the voices of young Jewish children doing calisthenics and generally preparing themselves for transfer to the public schools, which usually took place within six months. In the afternoons, the building vibrated with the sounds of after-school religious classes, domestic science classes for girls, clubs, and gym work. Once night fell there were classes in English, American history, geography and government,

sewing, bookkeeping, music, art, and gym for the adults of
the community. With every passing hour and in every
activity there was but one aim for those who ran the
institution: "the Americanization of the immigrant."[11]

The Educational Alliance defined itself as an institution
that was "both American and Jewish." All of its activities
were to serve as "mediators between immigrant and
American ways of living," and, according to Alliance
historian S. P. Rudens, bring about a "fusion which was to
the advantage of both."[12] But while the Alliance advertised
such lofty aims, in truth it was an organization run by the
rich (Jacob Schiff, Isaac Guggenheim, Isidore Straus, et al.)
for the refinement or containment of the poor. A *New York
Times* editorial of November 30, 1900 spoke of the
Alliance building as a "center of civilization in parts of
town that are most given over to savagery."[13] People were
urged to contribute to Alliance fund drives as a way of
insuring their way of life against their barbaric relatives. By
1908 it was costing the Alliance $100,527 a year to provide
such protection, with sports and physical culture accounting for a goodly portion of the expenditure.[14]

The Board of Directors of the Educational Alliance,
taking their cues from Jacob Riis and Charles Stover, and
later from leaders of the Playground Association of America like Luther Gulick and Joseph Lee, saw play as an
integral part of character development and a key to the
fashioning of a good citizen. The board and the staff
believed in other programs besides sports: they believed in
and established model flats for girls where they could
"cultivate a taste for those domestic virtues that tend to
make home-life happier and brighter"[15] and where the girls
could learn how to avoid becoming "a mere tenement
drudge";[16] the board believed in summer camps where these
rough-and-tumble city kids could get some fresh air and
stretch their legs; and the Alliance sponsored clubs where
the habits of democratic virtues were to be sown. But none
of the Alliance programs or strategies was treated more
seriously than sports for males:

> The importance of physical training for our down-town
> brethren cannot be overestimated. Our co-religionists are
> often charged with lack of physical courage and repugnance

to work. Nothing will more effectually remove this than athletic training.[17]

This description by the German Jews of the Alliance characterizing the East European Jew as unathletic and in need of special training and guidance became a rationale for the existence of programs designed to provide such aid. Gym classes became mandatory, athletic competitions between the Alliance and other settlements were arranged, and street play was organized under the supervision of Alliance personnel. In some ways this effort by the Alliance was of great benefit to the immigrant, who was in need of sporting equipment, training, and instruction. But in other ways and for other people the Alliance programs were anything other than helpful; in fact, they were condescending when they were not outright misdirected. Charles Stein, whose boyhood and young adult life was spent on the Lower East Side, remembers this about the Alliance:

> My feeling has been from the very start that it created an atmosphere, consciously or not, of welfare—looking down on the immigrant as though they had certain obligations to help him uplift himself, not accepting him as an equal....[18]

Bernarr MacFadden, publisher-editor of the widely read magazine *Physical Culture*, did not share the Alliance's view of the East European Jewish child. He observed of the Jewish male adolescent:

> His amusements, such as they are, are still more or less in line with those of the physical culturist. During the summer, the East River being handy, he leads a semi-aquatic existence. He haunts the docks and piers and in the intervals of diving off string pieces, takes long and luxurious sunbaths....[19]

He went on to note that such a child lived "in the street as much as possible. This may not be good for his manners, perhaps, but it is excellent for his health."

But the Alliance and the other settlements were less concerned about playing than they were concerned about having children play the "proper way." As A.H. Fromerson, editor of the English Department of the *Jewish Daily News*, put it:

The settlements have conspired with the big city to rob the
boy of his inalienable right to play: the city by means of
ordinances and prohibitions; the settlement by means of sit-
up-straight-and-be-good social rooms, literature clubs, civic
clubs, basket-weaving and scroll-iron works.[20]

The Commission of 1894

Settlement houses, like the Alliance, were to be outposts
of culture and civilization amid the squalor of Harlem,
Little Italy, and the Lower East Side. Sponsored by the rich
and operated by their offspring and middle-class social
workers, the settlements participated in the progressive
struggle for urban reform while they ran domestic science
classes for young women, reading classes for immigrants,
conducted sports leagues, sponsored lectures, and generally
ran programs for cultural or moral "betterment." One of the
first reforms to be taken up by the settlements as led by the
University Settlement in 1891 was "their campaign for
adequate play space,"[21] the settlement seeing itself—and
striving to be seen—as "an extension of the all-too-scant
home equipment of the neighborhood."[22]

What was the "home equipment of the neighborhood"?
Information was forthcoming from two sources: the muck-
raking of journalists like Jacob Riis, and public commissions of inquiry like the Tenement House Commission
of 1894. As Riis wrote in his highly acclaimed *How the
Other Half Lives*:

> In a room not thirteen feet either way slept twelve men and
> women, two or three in bunks set in a sort of alcove, the rest
> on the floor. A kerosene lamp burned dimly in the fearful
> atmosphere, probably to guide other and later arrivals to
> their "beds" for it was only just past midnight. A baby's
> fretful wail came from an adjoining hall-room, where in the
> semi-darkness three recumbent figures could be made out.
> The "apartment" was one of three in two adjoining buildings
> we had found within half an hour, similarly crowded.[23]

Riis also noted the political ramifications of such housing:

> The tenements had bred their Nemesis, a proletariat ready
> and able to avenge the wrongs of their crowds.[24]

Thus, the Tenement House Commission, chaired by the genteel editor of *Century Magazine* Richard Watson Gilder, entered its work fully conscious of the class dimensions of its assignment. It investigated the living conditions of more than a quarter of a million people and was "shocked to discover" such abominable overcrowding and unsanitary conditions. Only 306 persons of those investigated "had access to bathtubs in their homes," and only 51 dwelling units in a district housing a population of 121,323 "contained private toilets."[25] A portion of the Eleventh Ward on the Jewish Lower East Side "was among the most crowded spots on earth with a density per acre of 986.4 in 1894," according to the commission. The average tenement apartment rented for slightly more than the combined average income of its occupants. Yet amid all this anguish, filth, and tribulation, the commission could do no more than recommend the construction of "at least two parks in the Lower East Side and the completion of three more," in addition to suggesting the construction of school playgrounds and the dispersal of immigrants to the suburbs through rapid transit. Lubove notes:

> The Committee's concern over the deficiency of park and recreation facilities in tenement districts was its PRINCI-PLE CONTRIBUTION [sic] to neighborhood reconstruction. They hoped to enrich the life of the tenement dweller by introducing such rare treasures in the tenement neighborhood as fresh air, grass and playgrounds.[26]

This effort at "enrichment" came with massive propaganda and a call for the construction of two parks within three years. In a letter to the *New York Times* just after the commission had completed its work, Chairman Gilder urged

> that the whole matter [of parks and playgrounds] should be more carefully studied by the proper authorities and that there should be less accident and individual initiative and more system and science in the selection of park spaces adapted especially to what may be called the neighborhood needs of the masses of our people.[27]

The first call for consolidation, systematization, and

rationalization had been sounded; what remained to be
developed was the organizational framework for the actual-
ization of these ideas. The Outdoor Recreation League was
born out of just such a purpose.

The Outdoor Recreation League

As a result of the agitation for playgrounds and small
parks created by the Tenement House Commission of
1894, a law was passed appropriating $3 million to
purchase and construct small parks in the ghetto. At that
time, New York City had fifty parks, but a large percentage
of them could be reached only by railroad.[28] As recreation
historian Richard Knapp has shown, opportunities for
active use of the parks in ghetto areas were minimal.[29]

In 1897, the site committee appointed by reform mayor
Strong released a report that pointed to the confluence of
tuberculosis, substandard housing, crime and inadequate
park space. In part it read:

> The streets themselves have been largely occupied by car
> tracks and new servitudes, so that it is dangerous as well as
> obstructive to traffic for the children to use them for games
> of any kind, without incurring the interference of the
> police. A sense of hostility between the children and the
> guardians of public order is thus engendered, leading to the
> growth of a criminal class and to the education of citizens
> who become enemies of law and order. Nothing can be
> worse than this state of affairs, whether regarded from a
> moral or economic point of view.[30]

The publication of this report provided the cement
needed to bring together dozens of organizations concerned
with improving the play conditions of the immigrants and
the working class. A coalition was formed and named the
Outdoor Recreation League. One of the first things on the
agenda was a campaign for the establishment of a public,
open-air gymnasium,[31] such as existed in Boston. Charles-
bank, as the Boston facility was known, "was patronized by
all classes" and provided a location "where the rising
generation can enjoy athletic exercises."[32]

However, a facility that would be patronized by all classes was not intended to eradicate class struggles but rather to contain them. Iron magnate and playground philanthropist Abraham Hewitt expressed the containment strategy while speaking about "the class problem" at a meeting of the University Settlement in 1898. After noting that there had never been a period in our history where there was "such a contrast between the rich class at the top and the very poor at the bottom of the social structure," Hewitt asserted that this gap "must be bridged over" and that the only way to do so involved "nothing more than a practical application of the Commandment that we shall love our neighbors as ourselves," deploying sympathy most among the children:

> Whatever else may happen, however many unhappy wretches may go down to the grave in misery, society must see to it that every child has a fair chance.[33]

Society, then, was to become the great umpire, standing above the class conflict and adjudicating the questions that could not be mutually agreed upon. The rules of the game—the sanctity of private property; the commoditization of land, labor, etc.; the legitimacy of class society itself—all these were to be accepted as "natural." What could be contested was the amount of responsibility each class had toward the other. Part of the responsibility articulated by Hewitt, and espoused by most of the groups that comprised the Outdoor Recreation League, was for society to provide parallel worlds of joy where the workers could realize "life, liberty and the pursuit of happiness."[34] This world of parks, playgrounds, and open-air gyms, would allow for the continued exploitation of millions of people in the workaday world, and create amusement as compensation.

"Hudsonbank"—the free, open-air gym outfitted with sand gardens, swings, a running track, and equipment; built as a result of months of shrewd propaganda and political machinations by Outdoor Recreation League's Executive Committee (Jacob Schiff, Nathan Straus, Riis, Gilder,

Hewitt et al.)*—was one such compensation. Seward and Hamilton Fish parks, which originally opened in 1899 and 1900 as mere parks but reopened as playgrounds in 1903, were two others.

Seward and Hamilton Fish Parks

Seward Park, which took eight years to acquire and construct, and Hamilton Fish Park, which took a mere five, were the first observable signs of a shift in the conception and nature of park space. These parks, which opened in 1899 and 1900, were conceived by the reformers as cultural islands in the midst of ghetto land, situated in the heart of the Lower East Side. They were to be the parks of the future, complete with exercise apparatus, lockers, and, of course, organized-play leaders. As people like Park Board secretary Willie Holly saw them, these two parks were the strands from which a whole new life for the community was to be woven.

But, in fact, the two parks were simply pockets in a vast stretch of tenement material. They were places where the unemployed gathered, the aged rested, and the children carried on games of low-level organization conducted under the auspices of an ORL play supervisor. The destitute would seek shelter and sleep on the park benches, and periodically the police would take to "cleaning out the parks" by rousting these sweatshop refugees from their slumber. A not-insignificant facet of these crackdowns was noted by the *New York Times* of September 9, 1900, when it mentioned that these selfsame "bums," while they slept through the night, "discussed with rare intelligence the politics of the day or read the papers" in the daylight hours. Thus, the "cleaning" had its political content, too.

In 1903 when the parks reopened as playgrounds, the "bums" were still *capn a schmooz* (catching some winks)

---

*The leaders of the ORL accomplished their objectives by planting articles in newspapers agitating for Hudsonbank and Seward Park, by publishing pages-long lists of penny contributors to its campaigns, and by circulating petitions printed in Yiddish and English for the masses below Fourteenth Street. These petitions were then used to "prove" the support for ORL policies among the immigrants.

and arguing politics, but the children in the park were kept determinedly too busy to notice. Each park had provisions for outdoor gym work, basketball, swings, slides, etc. Both had a running track, and Hamilton Fish had tennis courts. There were lockers and public baths for the masses, a girls' section (for the more "delicate sex"), and attendants (two at Seward, three at Hamilton Fish).[35] Vast crowds gathered inside and out while tournaments and pageants conducted by the city at Seward Park saw 20,000 children in attendance and 40,000 people crowding the streets surrounding the park.[36] But unfortunately for the leaders of the organized-play movement, appearances were not everything.

Some of the problems which surfaced at the opening of the parks in 1899 and 1900 reappeared in 1903. The *New York Times* account of June 2, 1900, for example, details how the dignitaries present at the dedication of Hamilton Fish Park were forced to stand well back from the platform "to avoid having their trousers legs pulled and their toes struck by mischievous boys below." Park Board secretary Willie Holly suffered the assault of small boys who stuck pins into his "extremities during [his] presentation speech." Six policemen were needed to guard the grandstand, and even their presence could not keep the brass horns from being filled "with paper balls and other artifices."

Three years later at both Seward and Hamilton Fish the conflict grew much more intense. The *Times* report on the Seward Park opening states that "the crowd of 20,000 children present took matters into their own hands." Mayor Low's car was climbed on, and despite the calming efforts of the "Star-Spangled Banner," a healthy contingent of police was needed to keep people in line.[37] During a basketball game between a Seward Park team and a team from Hamilton Fish two weeks earlier, the police "were not only pushed and shoved about by the crush of small boys in the rear (as they stood shoulder to shoulder to keep the playground clear), but were at various times unintentionally hit in the eye with the ball, tripped up and otherwise injured in their dignity by the players...."[38]

These acts were more than the pranks of mischievous

children. The working-class youths at the Seward and Hamilton Fish Park ceremonies were defending their turf against encroachment by upper-class outsiders. Many of these children had been cigar workers from the age of five onward.[39] Thousands of them had to help with the economic struggles of their families by doing "homework" (factory work done in the home) or by *shlepping* (carrying) bundles of garment pieces to and from the contractor. The psychological impact of this oppression was severe. Veteran Lower East Side resident Freida Cohen remembers that "carrying the bundles" embarrassed her.[40] Harry Roskolenko remembers seeing his father at work in a factory: "Move this way, then that way. Pick up a cloak, spread it, press, grab, hold, hand—then do it over again. When I saw my father at it, I saw everything."[41]

In addition to being conscious of class and exploitation through a direct relationship to the process of production, children developed an awareness of the class struggle through the milieu of the Lower East Side—the parks where radicals rapped out their critiques, the grocery store credit books that "naturally" appeared when a strike was on,[42] the gloom and despair of the slack season. The various institutions in their lives—the schools, the sweatshops, and now the playgrounds—combined to create and perpetuate their feelings of oppression. Through these institutions they were denied autonomy and spontaneity. And even children as young as seven and eight came to recognize that this land of great promises was not all it had been advertised to be. They developed what social critic George Lukacs has labeled "a practical understanding of reification" and responded with "practical critical activity"[43] accordingly. Some, like Ben Levine, used words to slap back and poke fun at America—"Oh say can you see," he sang to the national anthem, "...any bedbugs on me?" Others attacked the most visible symbols of the system— the mayor, the monkeys-on-wheels, the parks authorities— with spitballs, pins, and verbal taunts. Still others engaged in prohibited sports activities. While the authorities' organized games were in progress, the open-air gymnasium at Seward Park, for example, was closed to the public. But, as the *Times* reported, "there was never a moment in the course of the day that the apparatus was not in use for 'stunts' that won as much applause from the crowd as did the best efforts of the rival teams devoted to ball games."[44]

Thus, many of the children of the community rejected the alienated activities and intense rivalries being called fun and play by the play directors and supervisors. They had their own ideas of happiness and skill, which they exhibited in their own ways at their own games. From the cigar factories to the sweatshops to the long lines of the unemployed, they came to know only too well the degradation of the life planned for them by the powerful, and in many cases they wanted no part of it.

The Public Schools

But, unfortunately for the immigrants, the organized-play movement got stronger and more popular. While the Outdoor Recreation League sponsored model facilities like Hudsonbank and Seward Park Playground, the public schools began to assume responsibility for some recreational activities previously handled by various charity organizations or not handled at all. In 1898 it was clear that the public school system was moving in the direction advocated for it by the elite social reformers. On the one hand it was centralizing the decision-making process in the hands of a superintendent of schools, while on the other hand it was developing a system of vacation schools and playgrounds under the direction of reformer and Playground Association director Seth T. Stewart.[45] These playgrounds and vacation schools were to be adjuncts and antidotes to the formal school program. While the decisions about hiring, textbooks, and curricula were passing from the control of the local school boards, the teachers, and the members of the various immigrant communities in New York City, the amount of control and importance held by the schools was increasing. People like Nicholas Murray Butler of Columbia University, Felix Warburg of the YMHA, and Julia Richman were using their prestige and power as members of the Public Education Association to disenfranchise the immigrant by "taking the school out of politics." Through nearly total control of New York City newspapers and editorials, they defined the problem of schooling in such a way as to make their solutions seem self-evident. This solution included playgrounds.

It included playgrounds and vacation schools for reasons of economy and control. The economy was to be had through savings in expenditures for police, courts, prisons, and in increased productivity by "playground-trained children" who learned industrial skills (raffia work, "something of tools," domestic science), and industrial discipline (scheduled play activities, etiquette, respect for authority). The control came about when children stepped onto the playgrounds and were greeted by play supervisors or teachers whose job it was to "inculcate the classic bourgeois virtues...cleanliness, politeness, formation of friendships, obedience to law, loyalty, justice, honesty, truthfulness, determination...."[46]

Initially, all playgrounds were, as Isidore Kanowitz pointed out, "for the better class," or at least for those quickest to identify with the upper class. Access in some cases depended on one's desire for salvation (in one of the early model playgrounds run by copper heiress Mabel Dodge, children had to line up outside the gate and declare, "I want to play!") or willingness to accept control (a child could be dismissed for bad conduct). However, by 1902 the city had assumed responsibility for the playgrounds, hired 1000 teachers to work there in the summer, and spent over $100,000 in Manhattan and the Bronx alone on seventy play sites.[47] A salary schedule and the requirement of a college degree or teaching experience for the play leaders was instituted, so that the impact of playgrounds could be expanded and extended, even to those in opposition to American capitalism. Ben Levine, whose father was a rabbi turned junk dealer by the American Dream, grew up in a Socialist household where love of the upper class and its institutions was certainly not the norm. Yet the playground (along with the library) escaped the bitter criticism of the bourgeoisie that usually came as a part of the family's discussions of Socialism "over tea with lemon on a side dish."[48] He recalls:

> There were signs all around that said the schools were open
> for vacation playgrounds. You went in and you sat down and
> they had game rooms where you got lottoes...and puz-
> zles....Actually there were wonderful things for kids to do.
> There were chalk talks where a guy told fairytales with
> colored chalk which was marvelous. Then you played
> indoor baseball, or softball they call it now. When you first
> came in the kids sat down in the yard and the fellow gave a
> chalk talk, sometimes. Or somebody organized teams for
> softball.

He didn't specifically remember the procedure for the flag
salute, but did recall that there were things like that you
had to do "to pay your dues."[49]

On the vacation playground you paid your dues in more
ways than one, but nevertheless the schools were extremely popular. In only their second year of operation
there were 15,000 applicants for only 5000 positions.[50]
Most people would have agreed with Ben in his praise of
the programs, seeing the playgrounds or vacation schools
as escapes from the harsh discipline of the schoolroom
proper, the exploitation of child labor, or the wrath of a cop
or neighborhood merchant who did not want any street
games to continue. All three of these items needed to be
fled from at one time or another, and if the playground was
not "dues-free," neither was it as expensive as the cost in
anguish or accident of the others. There were peers with
whom to joke and play; there was equipment to use; there
were occasional outings and extravaganzas to break whatever monotony might set in. But, in capitalism, what you
see *ain't* what you get, pop songs or not. What the immigrant children of New York City and the other millions of
children across the country saw in the organized play of the
playgrounds was some form of freedom; what they got was
its opposite.

They got what a group might be expected to receive
when it has been characterized by one of its leading benefactors, Abraham Hewitt, as potential plunderers of the
status quo. In a speech before the Annual Meeting of the
Educational Alliance in 1900, Hewitt declared that charity,
education, and support for programs aimed at the poor by
the rich was simply "building for their own protection."

Without such building, "barbarism, anarchy and plunder
will be the inevitable result." His admonitions of "a social
cataclysm unparalleled in history" were treated as serious
news by the *New York Times*, which carried the story
under the headline "Mr. Hewitt Predicts Disaster for the
Rich" on page 1.[51] The children of the playgrounds got sex-
segregated play—boys got athletics, girls received activities; boys used space, girls were under the shade; boys were
taught to overcome obstacles, girls grew to grace. They got
mathematized and systematized experience. They got football and flags, lottos and lice checks, tournaments and
talks by the play leader. In short, they got caught up in a
system which downplayed individuality and emphasized
conformity.

In addition to surrendering their spontaneity in sports
and games, the children were encouraged to cast off their
immigrant tongue, their folklore and fairytales. In the vacation schools and playgrounds the play leaders tried to color
in the gap between reality and the future with shades
selected from their (rather than the immigrants') color
schemes. Storytelling and censorship were key aspects of
this drive to disconnect immigrant children from immigrant traditions. A recommendation by the Playground
Association of America to its play leaders on this topic is
instructional:

> The child learns in but one way, by responding in his own
> activity to the thing he wishes to be. By means of the imagi-
> nation the child forms a mental picture which he holds in
> mind and strives to imitate. Therefore the most vital pur-
> pose of the story is to give high ideals which are reproduced
> in character. In consequence, it is of the utmost importance
> that the story shall have at its heart a spiritual truth, or, in
> other words, that it shall have a right virtue.[52]

Right virtues included all those that could be gleaned from
stories such as *Cinderella* (female passivity), *The Tales of
Sir Walter Scott* (male chivalry and aggression), Shake-
speare (valor, respect for authority), and Homer (love of the
"classics"). Since every playground run by the Board of
Education had a library and reading room, it is easy to see
that storytelling and "virtue infusion" were considered an

important part of the playground curriculum and were used to supplement the industrial training work, in-place games, music, and of course sports.

The Public Schools Athletic League (PSAL)

The PSAL was founded in 1903 by General Wingate and Luther Gulick to "discourage athletic work by the few and solely for athletics." It intended to "improve by proper games and physical training exercises, the physical condition of every student."[53] The league was intended to supplement and not supplant the physical education programs officially sponsored by the schools, but there was hardly any comparison between the two programs. As education historian Selma Berrol notes:

> Many schools did not teach physical education, for example, even though the cramped classrooms and inadequate play space of the tenement district cried out for such activities; or if they taught at all, the exercises consisted of marching around the school yard under the watchful eye of the teacher or doing calisthenics in class.[54]

The *New York Times* noted that the 100,000-boy league was "in measure, the outgrowth of the military organization movement that General Wingate fostered in the schools some years ago...."[55] But Wingate's motives and leadership, although he was a member of the Board of Education, were of lesser import than the designs held by Gulick.* These designs included using interscholastic sports to "awaken to consciousness" school loyalty and patriotism,[56] foster morality among the adolescents (especially the immigrants), and develop "efficient bodies,"[57] among other things. All three goals can best be understood as part of a larger whole, namely the PSAL athletic badge test and "the festival."

---

*According to his biographer, "No religious missionary has been more sincere in his aim to gather to Christ than Luther Gulick in his twofold objective of educating for character and bringing to Jesus" [Ethel Dorgan, *Luther Halsey Gulick, 1865–1918* (New York: Teachers College Press, 1934), p. 26]. His pursuit of these goals was consistent with the YMCA's Social Gospel and the missionary heritage within which he was raised. But Gulick's translation of the message of Christ into the language of physical education was nothing short of extraordinary. He was director of physical education at the YMCA College; the first director of physical

The PSAL athletic badge test was the result of Gulick's penchant for quasi-scientific experimentation, and his interpretation of the demands of an industrializing nation. The "science" of these tests and Gulick's psychological profile are discernible from the experiments he designed as a "value-free" physical educator. At different times Gulick "turned a hose on a sitting hen to see how soon she would desert the nest," as a measure of maternal affection; "placed [a student] in a hot bath and nearly parboiled him," to analyze the effects of heat on body temperature; "cut a tendon in his hand to determine whether greater flexibility would thereby be gained."[58] These tests were the paradigms used to develop the badge tests which called for a child of ten or twelve to do a certain number of pullups, broad jump x number of feet and inches, and run a sixty-yard dash in the required time.

Process became unimportant; attainment was everything. The PSAL distributed status as a rationed and quantified commodity —bronze badges or buttons for athletes, and silver for exceptional performances. As in society at large, the egos of those who competed expanded and contracted according to athletic proficiency, with the self reduced to "bucks" or buttons. From 1903 on, hundreds of thousands of children learned about the former from the latter.

The league was a mammoth operation which at times took on the atmosphere of festival cum conglomerate. The first meet sponsored by the PSAL was held in Madison Square Garden and the expenses were born by "voluntary contributions."[59] Within two years the PSAL grew to include seventeen affiliated high schools, twenty-two district leagues, and thirty one elementary school associations.[60] More than 150,000 boys were entered in the various events and competitions, and 1162 buttons were awarded.[61]

Thus, the PSAL came to take on an importance well beyond a

---

education in the New York City public school system; editor of the *American Physical Education Review*; president of the American Physical Education Association; author of innumerable and widely circulated articles on physical education and exercise; a founder of the Boy Scouts and the Camp Fire Girls; and most important, he was the leading force behind the PSAL and the Playground Association of America. In these last two capacities he did more than any other person in the nation's history to shape the face of American sport, and through it, culture. Unfortunately, his leadership and insight more accurately reflected and reinforced the contradictions of capitalist society than it portrayed the transcendent beauty of God or games.

mere after-school activity; it became *the* vehicle for physical expression for thousands of children. The city recognized that this was so when it appropriated half a million dollars for the league in 1905 (the money was used for the construction of four athletic fields outfitted with quarter-mile tracks and baseball–football fields).[62] The festival atmosphere was procured by awarding expensive trophies (one, donated by one of the "Dodge Girls," cost over $300),[63] the erection of stands to accommodate spectators, and the use of flags and bunting for championships. All this was for the purpose of realizing Gulick's vision of the "proper use of free time."[64] About festival days he wrote,

> They are great possessions which we are allowing to go to waste. They could be made the focal point of large streams of social life...and...render them educational.[65]

But education for Gulick meant really only one thing—repression, both external and internal in nature. According to him, the child should learn that obedience is expected at school and in the home:

> It is not his to say when he will study geography...what shall be the school hours....These must be settled by persons of far larger viewpoint than he possesses....The school must be fundamentally a monarchy; [and without obedience,] there is no true home.[66]

Even more important than obedience were the concepts of self-sacrifice and self-control. Gulick saw urbanization, specialization of the labor force, and commodity exchange as "inevitables":

> The last century has seen thrust upon it a set of fresh burdens of an extent, complexity, and character that have been unprecedented. These new needs must be and are being met by changes in the direction of the development of consciousness.[67]

This consciousness was to be molded through the deployment of sandpiles, for kindergarteners; playgrounds, for young children; and athletic fields, for adolescents:

> Upon them rests the development of that self-control which is related to an appreciation of the needs of the rest of the group and of the corporate conscience, which is rendered necessary by the complex interdependence of modern life.[68]

As will be seen later, this analysis was based on the psychology of G. Stanley Hall, who perceived the development of the child as the ontological recapitulation of the history of the human race. Now, it is important to note that these beliefs were part of the basic assumptions about life held by Gulick and that the shape of the PSAL (as well as the PAA, Boy Scouts, and Camp Fire Girls) was informed by such ideas. The development of "corporate conscience," self-realization as "the most perfect sinking of one's self in the welfare of the larger unit," the appropriateness of self-sacrifice, all these were to be learned as part of the "mutual-consent kind" of control fostered by the PSAL and playgrounds.[69] This control had as its ideological premise the idea of freedom. "The child is free to leave [it] if he chooses," wrote Gulick.[70]

On closer examination, however, the idea of freedom was more fiction than fact, and the need for self-sacrifice had more to do with the needs of capital than with the welfare of the larger unit. Gulick's "take it or leave it" pitch was similar to the free-contract theory which had been expounded for decades as a defense of the wage-labor system.

As Marx noted about the freedom of wage-labor, you were free—either to sell yourself or starve. Since the worker had lost control of the productive process, he was free only in the distorted sense of the word. Similarly the child, who had been denied opportunities for physical expression in the school and whose autonomous street world filled with play/games and sport had been increasingly coming under assault by the police and the reformers, had also been removed from the control of sports production (access to space, equipment, nonutilitarian time). His/her freedom was the choice of playing ball "our way or not at all." And just as the threat of confinement for pauperism or arrest at the picket line was held as a threat over those who defied the wage-labor system, coercion—in the form of arraignment before the children's court or harassment by the police—could be the fate of uncooperative youngsters. To a child, the ramifications of going afoul of the law were a part of the terrorism of everyday life. Ben Levine remembers:

> Sometimes the police would chase you [while playing ball in the street], and they would take your name which scared me like anything. They always took your name. So we always looked out for them.[71]

Gulick was not ignorant of the relationship between his beliefs and the perpetuation of capitalist relations. He knew that this "complex interdependence of modern life" rested on a base of exploitation, but that was of little consequence. "This exploitation," he wrote in *A Philosophy of Play*, "is neither good nor evil." It simply demanded adaptation and that which had served the capitalist in the workplace was to be extended to a world view encompassing both play and work. Simply put, his ideology was "Trust those who have successfully made sense (and dollars) from the chaos of the times." Gulick even went so far as to interpret the demands of self-control into the language of physical comportment and carriage: "It is necessary that he [the pupil or athlete] resolutely hold his body in the desired position; this needs to be impressed with great vigor and persistence."[72] Combined with the PSAL and playground prohibitions against swearing, spitting, and smoking, the dress codes, and bans on unsupervised intersexual play, these posture rules made for an almost total control of the behavior patterns of the youth of the immigrant working-class Jews.

Bureaus and Efficiency

From the Tenement House Commission of 1894 through to the institution of a Public Recreation Commission twenty years later, the movement for municipally sponsored, supervised, and coordinated playgrounds grew geometrically. In the first fourteen years of the organized play movement (1891–1905), the city purchased no less than eleven parks (including Seward, Hamilton Fish, and Corlears Hook on the Lower East Side) at a total cost of $14,511,600. In Manhattan, park area increased by 40 percent from 1890 to 1910,[73] and the park budget increased from $480,000 in 1899 to $1,385,488 in 1913.[74] The Park Board, the Department of Docks, the settlements, and the private play organizations were all operating play and recreation programs for the masses. By 1912 the Board of Education was running 124 vacation playgrounds and 33 evening recreation centers with an average nightly attendance of 12,175, whereas as late as 1900 the evening recreation centers numbered only eight with an average nightly attendance of 675, while the vacation playgrounds in 1898 numbered a mere thirty.[75] Yet, despite these increases, the organized-play movement was never able to keep up with immigration. Nor could it break free from its own class logic, which called for the commoditization of everything and which thus created land speculation as a barrier to meeting the real needs of those without play space. From 1890 onward, the ratio of acreage of park space per thousand residents in Manhattan, for example, decreased steadily. It went from 0.77 acres per thousand people in 1890 to 0.68 in 1900, 0.63 in 1910, and 0.58 in 1914.[76] A report by the Public Recreation Commission in 1912, for example, revealed that the Lower East Side had 237,222 children between the ages of six and fourteen and less than eighteen acres of play space. Only 6 percent of Manhattan children were reached by facilities offered by the Parks Department. The report called for the purchase and development of an additional 100 acres of parks which would provide play space for an estimated 140,000 additional children.[77]

Because the commission's suggestion to purchase more land was only one facet of its recommendations, and because the other suggestions were less costly to implement and less politically complicated than the purchase of land, public policy moved in a different direction—from acquisition to efficiency. Efficiency, as historian Samuel Haber points out, meant many different things to many different people, but for the reformers it "provided a standpoint from which...[those]...who had declared their allegiance to democracy could resist the leveling tendencies of the principle of equality. They could advance reform and at the same time provide a safeguard to the 'college-bred.'"[78] In the case of the movement for playground efficiency, that ideology not only provided a safeguard, but it insured that the resistance of the Lower East Side youth would be handled with dispatch.

The movement for efficiency beginning with the publication of two reports by the Rockefeller-funded Bureau of Municipal Research in 1908, was not without its merits. Because so many different organizations were responsible for providing recreation programs and facilities, there was a tremendous amount of bureaucratic waste and duplication. Certainly, if any of the stories that circulated about Tammany graft had any base in reality, the Park Board (which had its share of scandals involving contracts and kickbacks) could be identified as a likely culprit. But even granting the possibility of widespread corruption, the fact remains that the provisions were totally inadequate and no amount of cost analysis would ever change that. Still, the fight against waste and for efficiency, which also meant consolidation, went ahead full steam. With all the subtlety of a derrick in a courtyard, the Bureau of Municipal Research kicked off the play efficiency/consolidation campaign by announcing that the "administrative methods then employed were designed to waste funds." It went on to claim that

> Public provision for park needs in the past decade has been sufficiently generous to secure not only proper maintenance of park property, but a progressive beautification of park grounds. Thousands of dollars wasted by disorganized administration might long ago have been used to plant the mile of rhododendrons which now a grateful public receives from private benefaction.[79]

The bureau bemoaned the fact that the Park Board "has been devoted almost exclusively to the improvement of park property and little thought has been given to the problem of providing businesslike methods of administration."[80] In point of fact, of the thirty-seven significant defects in Park Board work listed by the bureau, all but three had to do with inefficient or defective accounting procedures or financial licensing. The bureau anguished that it was "impossible to tell the exact cost of maintaining the park system" in any year.[81] Thus, the bureau's goal became to "place on a business basis the administration of parks."[82] Within two years, a New York City Recreation Bureau was established and time sheets, inspections, and verified reports became as much a part of playground mechanics as play leaders.

If the consolidation of political power in the city over play programs and facilities was proceeding apace, at times complementing and at other times anticipating the municipalization of everyday life, there was another side to the picture that made the pace too slow for the leaders of organized play. That side was the immigrants' response to the efficiency of oppression and the oppression of efficiency. Indeed, the reports of the Recreation Bureau itself from 1910 onward are replete with accounts of vandalism, harassment, and petty theft directed against the parks and playgrounds, park authorities, and members of the immigrant group itself who had been recruited to act as guardians of the parks. The 1910 report had but one short sentence: "The damage done to park property from the thoughtlessness on the part of both children and adults is very great."[83] In the 1911 report, two sentences described the need to detail special laborers to guard park equipment at night. By 1913, the Department of Parks "Annual Report" noted that companies of "Auxiliary Boy Police" had been formed "to enforce the Department regulations and to prevent damage in the parks." Trees had been uprooted, shrubs pulled to pieces, bronze railings ripped off to be sold, lights smashed, and flagpoles broken. "The damage done during one season through vandalism," observed the report, "is almost incredible." And the "Auxiliary Police," equipped with badges and a written permit which authorized them to enforce the rules, were helpless. In fact, the wearers of the badges were "greatly harassed" and attacks on them "often resulted in adding to the damage to the parks rather than preventing it." Eventually, the ranks of the defenders "became depleted."[84]

Give them a chance for innocent sports,
Give them a chance for fun,
Better a playground plot than court
And a jail when the harm is done.
Give them a chance—if you stint them now,
Tomorrow you'll have to pay
A larger bill for a darker ill,
So give them a place to play.

—Denis A. McCarthy
The Playground, June 3, 1909

CHAPTER 4 # The Playground
Association of America

By 1905 almost everyone concerned with social reform was concerned with play and almost every reform organization was involved in assisting the rise of organized play in one form or another. The settlement houses, the Outdoor Recreation League, the vacation schools all shared some common perceptions about the nature of the New American City and some common fears about the radical political ideas that were being expressed there. Urbanization was thought to bring with it an unsafe and unhealthy atmosphere for children who needed playgrounds "to train the[ir] boundless energy...towards useful and loyal citizenship." The reformers fretted over "the hazard of the street where they [the children] are menaced on all sides by moral and physical dangers."[1] And they worried that "unless increasing opportunities for the enjoyment of leisure be opened to men as a right and not as a privilege, we shall soon have a large number of people who will not feel a loyalty to the United States."[2] Howard S. Braucher articulated a few years later what underlay that threat of disloyalty when he said, "the expenditure of tax funds for community centers [including playgrounds and vacation schools] is the best form of insurance against assassination and social revolution."[3]

But if it were true that by 1905 most of the reformers shared these fears and had begun to do something about the dangers of unregulated play, it was also true that their efforts were uncoordinated and incomplete. Luther Gulick, who was intimately aware of the problems of unorganized play and unorganized reform efforts in his capacity as the first director of physical education for New York City, and Henry Curtis, who viewed the same problems from his post as supervisor of playgrounds on the Lower East Side, shared a conviction that a national movement to promote American forms of play was necessary if the problems of the Lower East Side were not to engulf the nation. In 1906, they founded the Playground Association of America, with the goal of building a national, coordinated, and systematic play movement.

The association got off to a great start but soon faltered. Its initial meeting in Washington, D.C., in 1906 was attended by leaders of the organized-play movement from around the country. They met for five days, from April 10 through April 15, and emerged from their discussions with a plan for the Playground Association of America, as well as an invitation to the White House from President Teddy Roosevelt. Roosevelt agreed to become the honorary president of the organization, Jane Addams was elected vice-president, and Luther Gulick, president. With such auspicious leadership, the association seemed to have nothing but clear sailing ahead, but it floundered for lack of money. Even though its leaders were prestigious, its members were predominantly social workers, educators, and physical education specialists whose resources, though not inconsiderable, were inadequate for the vast undertaking charted by Gulick, Addams, and Curtis. Experience had proven that looking to the immigrants themselves for financial support would be futile even though they were to be the beneficiaries of the association's efforts. In 1899 the Lower East Side Recreation Society had appealed to the young and old of the Lower East Side for funds for play programs and that appeal netted a mere $105, most of which came from nonresidents. Millionaire Isidor Straus, the coordinator of the appeal, was thus moved to say, "There was almost a total lack of faith or sympathy"[4] among the people for this fund drive. With this option of raising money from the impoverished immigrants precluded, the association undertook to raise funds from interested patrons and in its first year it collected $2164 toward its operating expenses. This amount, while quite small for the budget of a national organization, was enough to allow for the development of *The Playground*, the association's journal which made its first appearance in April 1907 and which played a crucial role in the organization's success.

The Playground played an important role for the Playground Association of America and for the organized-play movement as a whole. The rise of organized play had passed through the stage of alienating the child from control of his or her sports through the passage of antistreet play laws and the organization of play throughout the neighborhood by settlements, schools, and the city. The movement was now involved in the creation of an ideology that would justify its control of play based on its superior understanding of the science of play, play facilities, and equipment. Information was crucial and *The Playground* was to be instrumental in developing and disseminating that information. The very first issue of the journal conveyed this intent when it listed as the association's purposes:

1. The *study* of playground construction and administration and experimentation with new features.
2. Collection in a library and museum all the available *knowledge* on the subject of play.
3. Publication and dissemination of *information* on playgrounds through magazines, conventions and classes.
4. Registration and account of trained playground workers and the facilitation of filling vacancies for municipalities seeking such persons.[5]

With Gulick, *The Playground*, and a very successful and well-attended Recreation Congress in New York in 1907 paving the way, the association was able to attract some financial support from the Russell Sage Foundation, which paid Gulick's salary and made contributions to the PAA in 1908 and 1909. But it was not until late in 1909, with the ascendancy of millionaire Joseph Lee to the presidency, that the PAA became a viable national organization.[6] Under his leadership, and because of his financial connections and contributions, the association was able to employ a larger staff including field secretaries, undertake the preparation of "The Normal Course of Play,"[7] and design a program for the professionalization of play leaders.

With a more solid financial base, the association was able to develop new techniques of service, and in this line it hired Lee F. Hanmer, an inspector of athletics in the New York public schools, as its first field secretary. The field secretary became a sort of utility infielder for the Playground Association of America, going from city to city both to collect and to disseminate information about playgrounds. In his first year with the PAA, Hanmer traveled throughout the country and solicited information from cities with populations of over 5000. His was a position that demanded flexibility and savvy, as the groundwork for his rights or responsibilities had not yet been laid. This was, of course, true of the association in general and the reform movement as a whole. Social work had heretofore existed as local institutions with ties to particular constituencies, clientele, and benefactors.[8] The upper class had only recently started to develop a national cogency and consciousness, paralleling the development of national spheres of production and distribution by the trusts. Increasing immigration, which peaked in 1905,[9] provided the negative incentive for national cogency. When coupled with the consolidation of capital, this led to the founding and expansion of organizations like the National Civic Federation, the immigrant restriction leagues, and the Playground Association of America. Hanmer's fieldwork and the fieldwork of subsequent secretaries can be taken as a valuable indication of the developing coordination skills and programs of the elite. Such work reveals both the ideology and strategy of a class in the process of consolidating its power and influence.

These traveling salespeople known as field secretaries were also referred to as "Play Efficiency Engineers,"[10] and they were responsible for spreading the play message in whatever way the association deemed proper. At first Lee Hanmer was merely charged with corresponding with cities that were curious about properly equipping and organizing individual playgrounds. As the work of the association progressed, emphasis shifted from developing and financing play facilities to coordinating the training of play directors and the integration of the municipalities' play programs.

Each field secretary was thoroughly briefed and issued instructions on how to secure the assistance of the local elite. This was not always a simple task. In New York City, the immigrant/radical threat was understood by the Schiffs, Warburgs et al., to require a defense focused on the children. Jacob Schiff, Felix Warburg, and Isidor Straus, for example, were prime benefactors of such institutions as the Educational Alliance, the YMHA, and the Public Education Association. Both Schiff and Warburg served as honorary vice-presidents of the Playground Association of America's Fourth National Recreation Congress, and they were often called on to sponsor this or that event by other members of the organized-play movement.[11] At the Second National Recreation Congress, Felix Warburg expressed his happiness over the fact that:

> Now large numbers of young people spend their evenings in healthy rivalry in these centers [playgrounds and gyms] and go home, perhaps the proud winner in some friendly competitions. Boys going home in such a happy frame of mind are not apt to loiter in the streets and to fall victims of gangs and *other bad influences* [emphasis added].[12]

This understanding of the connection between playgrounds and the prevention of social and political problems caused by urbanization, immigration, and industrialization was slower in coming to elites in cities where these factors and the threat of Socialism were less pressing:

> Duluth [Minn.] seems to be a good deal like several other cities which I have visited in the fact that many of its leading business men are cautious, conservative, unfamiliar with social service and inclined to scrutinize a proposition very hard until they are convinced that it is sound.[13]

As a way of convincing, two techniques were used. One
involved appealing to the more humanitarian instincts of
the prospective donor, the other relied on the sense of propriety that could be cultivated by the prodding of the field
worker. In the first technique, the association would mail
to local leaders "human interest press releases" with the
quotes of street-car conductors, janitors, the man next door,
a mother, and a boy who "tell what they think of neighborhood playgrounds." These quotes would be packaged with
six "true stories" about children who had stopped whining,
sailed boats, and learned team play as a result of playgrounds made possible "through contributions to the Playground Association of America."*[14] The second strategy
involved personal contact made by the field worker with
local ministers, "key people," and businessmen. Finally, the
association suggested (in a forty-page pamphlet) how to
gain support for the play movement by contacting the local
Chamber of Commerce or the mayor. All three of these
methods were to be used as a wedge toward calling a
meeting of the local elites and developing committees for
fundraising. What the recreation secretaries did not want
was the active participation at the planning stage of the
very people for whom the recreation facilities were
intended. This is revealed by the suggestions of one of the
three field workers:

> In planning this meeting, I feel that it is most important to
> keep it from resolving itself into an unwieldly "mass meet-
> ing" at which it would be almost impossible to secure defi-
> nite action. While, strictly speaking, the meeting should be
> public, the character of the group may be shaped by avoid-
> ing too much publicity and by concentrating efforts on the
> people whose cooperation is most needed. "Instead of a
> schoolhouse," a meeting in a "private house" is "more effec-
> tive" in securing the presence of substantial, resourceful
> citizens.[15]

The Playground Association of America put great faith
and financial resources into the work of the field staff.

---

*The Playground Association of America became the Playground and
Recreation Association of America, and is now the National Parks and
Recreation Association. For convenience, I refer to the PAA throughout.

Recreation historian Richard Knapp describes their work as "perhaps the most successful method used by the Association to disseminate the concept of public recreation." At one time, the budget for field services came to $58,557, a staggeringly high proportion of the total budget of only $82,506.[16] The field workers paid back that confidence by organizing year-round recreation systems between the years 1912 and 1916. They made organizational visits to help establish a pushing committee "whose definite object is getting a recreation secretary or to gain the cooperation of some existing organizations having genuine influence." They conducted follow-up visits, inspection visits, and in general acted as standardizers of recreation programs, applying the ideology of the PAA even into the recesses of language where they strove for linguistic hegemony: "The Association feels that it will help materially in the work of the country if we can succeed in having the same names for the various recreation positions used throughout the country." It also counselled on using the word "community" and not "social," a "playground with play leaders 'instead of supervised playgrounds' because 'men and women do not like to think of being supervised.'"[17]

The PAA not only supervised and suggested, but it became the recognized authority in the field. By 1913, the Playground Association of America had nine field and two associate secretaries in the cities and towns of America. These play missionaries coordinated fundraising, offered advice on equipment, and even went so far as to interpret the personal feelings and desires of the children the playground system was to serve. In the matter of equipment, a gap was assumed to exist between what the children wanted (merely an opportunity to play) and what the adults knew was best for them (a fully equipped playground with a play leader). E. B. DeGroot, the general director of playgrounds in Chicago, whose pamphlets on the subject of equipment were carried by the field secretaries to the cities they visited, wrote:

> I believe that the vast majority of children were perfectly content with their present play opportunities and facili-

ties....[The problem is] one of presenting certain play areas in every community, so thoughtfully and perfectly equipped that they will attract and hold the children.[18]

The perfectly equipped surroundings included such items as night lighting, graded and loamed land, shaded, tree-lined sections, toilets, fountains, fences, flag poles with American flags, bulletin boards, and more.

The Communication of Cooptation

If the allure of a playground "pimping" for the proper use of leisure time was not enough for the effective cooptation of the children who otherwise would "pick up their play as they go,"[19] then the field secretaries, whose class background made them as remote from the life experiences of the children as that of the settlement workers (mostly college-bred sons and daughters of money), would have to develop even more refined techniques. One such move involved the administration of self-reports by the children targeted as potential playground users, reports as to what they were currently doing with their "free time." The cooperation of school superintendents was sought, and teachers were asked to have their charges write "informal letters telling what they do outside of school hours upon a definite day or days":

> Explain clearly that the letters are not to be marked for grammar, spelling or any other feature, that their purpose is to find out what the young folks of _____ are doing in their leisure hours and what they would like to do. The purpose is to help the playground recreation movement.[20]

Thus, the children were to be given a reprieve from the authoritarian world of school and the sovereign's control over communication—the rules of language being temporarily suspended so that the insides of the student could be made available to the play organizers. Although it often took as long as two weeks for the responses to be tabulated, the results justified such patience. For when the students cooperated, the organizers took advantage of this "naïveté" and used the information gathered against the informers. Playgrounds were built and laws against playing in the streets were passed. Children from Scranton, Pennsylvania, to Detroit, Michigan, were plotted, packaged, and had their spontaneity purloined under the guise of giving them what they asked for.

Propaganda: Posters and the Press

From the time of its promotion to the major leagues of capital, the organized-play movement and the Playground Association of America never suffered for lack of favorable publicity. Given the entrepreneurial nature and shared value system of publishers and people like playground financiers Jacob Schiff and Joseph Lee, this should not be surprising. What might astonish, however, is the incredible amount of calculation and machination that went into guaranteeing such support. Between 1894 and 1914, the *New York Times* and the *New York Herald Tribune* never expressed the slightest disagreement or disillusionment with the goals, philosophies, or ideology of the play movement in general and the PAA in particular. The annual play conferences and meetings of the local associations were all reported with the seriousness otherwise accorded major civic developments and organizations.

A second indication of the support given the play movement can be gleaned from the participation of papers in the organized leagues and games themselves. In New York City, the *Sunday World* sponsored hundreds of teams in its playground baseball league, while the *Herald* was affectionately known as "the playground newspaper" because it published the results and league standings of the games and teams. Outdoor bulletin boards were maintained at play sites on the Lower East Side and elsewhere, and the page of the paper that contained the "playground news" was duly posted.[21]

Another indication of the degree of harmony that characterized the play movement and the press is the coverage afforded the playground drive of 1908 in Massachusetts. At that time, the state papers in effect became the public relations arm of the PAA. Behind big and small headlines, in the letters to the editor, as well as on the news pages, the meaning of playgrounds for the salvation of civilization was heralded. An examination of the files of the National

Parks and Recreation Association reveals that at least fifteen articles and letters that appeared in Massachusetts
papers during the campaign were written by members of
the PAA. The articles were drafted as "press releases," but it
seems clear, given the remarkable similarity of the language between the release and the news copy, that neither
the PAA nor the publishers or editors treated them as anything less than straight copy.[22] Perhaps it was this "hospi-
tality" that led *The Playground* in September 1915 to
remark:

> Among the powerful friends of playgrounds and recreation
> in America, the newspapers of the country may be given an
> important rank, for few and scattered are the editorials
> against playgrounds, while the number of splendid, sane,
> endorsements in the editorial columns can scarcely be
> counted.[23]

The PAA built support for its ideology not only by
directly courting the press but by doing some indirect flirt-
ing as well. For example, part of the strategy for getting
good press involved having prominent citizens forward letters to other prominent people and the press, thus starting
a chain letter. Each letter would contain a piece of playground propaganda and would serve both to legitimize the
movement and to intimidate any editor who might have
thought otherwise about the urgency of playgrounds or
recreation systems. The idea of a propaganda campaign
such as this was announced in *The Playground* in 1909,[24]
and shortly thereafter "form letters and sheets" were prepared to minimize the effort and clarify the goals to which
Carnegie, Morgan, et al., would lend their names. Typically,
a prospective endorser would be sent a three-page sheet
that contained all the clichés being used to hype the play
movement. The sheet asked, "Are you willing to give us in
a few words the reason why you believe in the playground
movement? May we quote your statement?" The clichés followed, and the supporter was asked to "mark 1, 2, 3, 4 before
the appeals which seem to you strongest." The first two
appeals appear below:

1. Dependency. "The boy without a playground is father to the
   man without a job." *Joseph Lee*

2. Delinquency. "The presence of recreation centers in the South Side of Chicago was coincident with a decrease of delinquency within a radius of a half mile of the centers of 28.5%. Over a much larger area than the one-half mile radius, the recreation centers decreased delinquency 17%." *Allen T. Burns, Dean of the Chicago School of Civics and Philanthropy, 1908.*[25]

Other appeals listed included street accidents, health and physical efficiency, tuberculosis, industrial efficiency, progress, moral character, citizenship, patriotism, individuality, family unity, and community spirit.[26] Not even the bottled elixirs of the street-corner hucksters claimed to do so much for so little. A quick flick of the wrist and any personage could join the ranks of J.P., T.R., or the good doctor who said, "Recreation does for a city what vaccination does for an individual.... It is truly an antitoxin for many of the inherent maladies of city life as a serum is for smallpox."[27] A quick flick of the wrist and space, time, and situations would become interchangeable, all parts of the larger unit of playground propaganda. Adaptable articles, interchangeable events, replaceable personages—all these were facets of the organized-play movement's strategic core. So complete was the effort to manipulate and control information and ideology that the PAA even developed a list of suggestions for playground posters. These were of the standard fare—quotes by Teddy Roosevelt, warnings about traffic accidents and TB, law and order messages.[28] Play associations were urged to use such posters as part of the campaign to eradicate "a lack of interest in the playground" by neighborhood people who are ignorant "of its objects and methods."[29]

The play associations believed in the idea that the "average citizen" needed to be "progressively educated to an appreciation of playground values and requirement." The association leaders evidently assumed that the organization or supervision of children's play would be considered "utterly foreign to the traditions and common sense" of the common man. They worked hard to eradicate this lack of interest, relying on the play leader as the front-line soldier in that battle.[30]

Interpretive Play Bosses

The year 1909 marked the birth of a new profession—
playground director. Before that time there were people
employed as directors, but the scope of their training was
limited, if not haphazard. From 1909 onward, under the
supervision of the PAA, the playground directors' concern
shifted from controlling the bodies of the children who
assembled on the playgrounds to capturing the hearts and
minds of the youngsters. Their training changed accordingly. Previously, play directors received little or no formal
instruction in anything other than games leadership; as
professionalization set in, they received a sophisticated
and lengthy education in the techniques of sociology and
psychology. This began in 1908–09 with the development
of "The Normal Course of Play." Developed by the PAA "to
provide a start toward systematic training of leaders to various levels of competence for service in the expanding field
of public recreation," it required that they learn such items
as "child nature" and "the nature and function of play," as
well as "practical conduct of a playground" and "organization and management of activities."[31] An article in *The
Playground* reflected the attitude and strategy of the
association toward the playground directors:

> The men and women employed for playground service,
> [therefore] should not be regarded as mere instructors, play
> bosses, or leaders of game, but rather as thoughtful
> managers, interpreters of child and adolescent life, chemists
> of human desires and captains of the marching legions of
> young people on the way to a "square deal" citizenship.[32]

The play directors were seen as the most important
pieces of equipment on the playground,[33] and their per-
sonalities were the primary consideration for obtaining a
position through the assistance of the PAA. Personality
was, of course, a word that could be subject to broad
interpretation, and so the association quickly rushed to fill
any gap that might destroy its definition:

> No person who is lacking in general refinement or pleasing
> ways or an appreciation of the social service to be rendered
> should be accepted under any circumstances for a play-

ground position. The judgment on this score should be based on apparent refinement, bearing, language, as shown in conversation and habits and character, as vouchsafed for by responsible acquaintances or employers.[34]

In order to insure that the proper refinement was given its due weight in assessing the qualified, a test was designed. It consisted of three equally weighted parts of personality, practice, and theory. In order to be given a positive rating, and therefore to receive the considerable help in finding employment that the association could and did give, a score of 70 was required and a candidate could not receive less than 20 points in any category and pass. Thus, a young man or woman of working-class origins without access to the recommendations and contacts of the middle or upper class was effectively disenfranchised from work on the playgrounds. The "thoughtful managers and interpreters of child and adolescent life" were those who either shared the beliefs and world views of the elite or were themselves members of that class.

What did these professional play supervisors want? How did they conceive of their role and the task of the playground? In the July 1909 issue of *The Playground*, one such play supervisor, John H. Chase, put it succinctly:

> We want a play factory; we want it to run at top speed, on schedule time, with the best machinery and skilled operatives. We want to turn out the maximum product of happiness....[35]

Turning out "the maximum product of happiness" was a rationalized process that bore a great similarity to the maximization of profit that is an inherent tendency of the capitalist mode of production. Just as modern management came into being on the basis of the demand by capital to consolidate its control and expand its horizon,[36] modern playground management arose to give order and internal logic to leisure production. Playground workers, like the members of management in the sphere of production, were classified in a hierarchy and given rights and responsibilities accordingly. They were:

1. System supervisors charged with site selection, planning, finances, outside relations, and staffing;

2. Head directors responsible for tasks such as instruction
   in games or industrial work, the administration of activities (selecting teams, providing first aid), the direction
   and control of conduct, and the care of equipment;
3. Assistants to the director who taught, guided, controlled,
   and organized;
4. Specialists like kindergartners, storytellers, librarians,
   visiting nurses, and industrial teachers; and
5. Janitors, mechanics, guards.

Not every city, quite naturally, was able to comply with
such an intense and potentially expensive division of roles.
In not every case were the directors people who had "at
least two years above the high school in a state normal
school or normal school of physical education or in a college"[37] as "The Normal Course of Play" and the PAA
recommended. But there were standards, and to the degree
that it was possible the association was intent on uphold-
ing them. In fact, the reformers were so concerned about
maintaining those standards that they were willing to lose
playground attendees more than they were willing to
sacrifice their ideals. Once, for example, in the Bronx, there
was a children's strike against the playground because of a
change in the leadership. "For two days" the striking
children "prevented all children from entering the playground." But the playground authorities would not give in
to this kind of squeeze play. They threatened the perma-
nent closing of the playground and the removal of all
equipment if the children did not relent and send a letter of
apology to the president of the New York Parks and
Playgrounds Association, Eugene Philbin.[38] This tactic paid
off, for the strike was broken and the strikers were called
out—or rather *into* the playground.

"The Normal Course of Play"

In 1908, Clark W. Hetherington was appointed chairman
of the Playground Association's committee for the "Normal
Course of Play."[39] Hetherington was a somber man, often
criticized even by his best friends as someone who "has
taken himself so seriously that...he has, to a large extent,

defeated his own purpose."[40] In a personal sense that assessment was probably true, but in a professional sense it was not. Hetherington was committed to establishing standards, compiling statistics, and separating information from intuition.[41] He brought to the position an intellectual commitment to play as the great reformer, having once stated after working in the Whittier Reformatory for boys, "My elaborate statistics showed that 80% of the inmates were in the institution because of the neglect of their play impulses."[42] Hetherington had been a graduate of Stanford, a fellow and assistant at Clark University where he studied under G. Stanley Hall, and a professor of physical education before he became a director of the PAA in 1906 and "Normal Course" chairman two years later. In that position he undertook to apply the lessons of bourgeois psychology and child study systematically to the training of play directors and recreation leaders.

The systematic approach followed by Hetherington and his committee was a perfect example of academic categorization gone wild. It included the interpretation and treatment of adult play as distinct from child's play; the division of study into three sections (one for professional playground directors, one for temporary employees, and one for those being trained in the normal schools in other subjects); and the division of the report into seven parts which included bits of psychology, playground movement history, management, first aid, and sociology.[43] Each of these categories was based on the tacit belief that the best way to understand, teach, and transmit information is to treat each fragment as a separate, isolated fact, thus precluding an understanding of the whole by the object (children) or the subject (play leaders).

This intense division of "The Normal Course" syllabus and its definitions made it impossible for children and working adults to keep abreast of and understand the latest developments in recreation and social control. There were only bits and pieces of information for them to grab and so they were hardly in a position to criticize the moves, although they might be suspicious of the organized-play leaders' motives. As in the workplace where each job was becoming more and more specialized, knowledge about play was becoming more detailed, specialized, and fragmented. The result was the defeat of the immigrant workers' holistic culture by atomized mass culture. Communities and play were divided and conquered.

The class logic of "The Normal Course of Play" included a discussion of the mental and physiological inferiority of women, race differences, and the child-study psychology developed by Hetherington's teacher G. Stanley Hall.[44] All these will be treated elsewhere. Of paramount importance now is an investigation of the technical aspects of the course because it was primarily in response to the lack of technical training in the normal schools that the course was developed. It was from that lack that the course drew its raison d'être.

Lest there be any confusion, Section 6 of "The Normal Course" set out to define a playground. Not surprisingly, the answer to "What is a playground?" was "a piece of land under the direction of a play director" whose responsibility it was to "secure the attendance of the children" and "keep it out of the hands of gangs."[45] A definition such as this fitted nicely into the designs of the reformers. For once a playground was defined as an institution in which responsibility for the proper conduct of the children fell to a play leader (often outnumbered by the children in ratios of dozens to one), it became only "natural" that a system of hierarchy and designated authority would be instituted. Thus, as an aid in organizing, "The Normal Course" advises:

> The Director will find it a great help in his work if he will select a few of the stronger and more reliable members of the playground as volunteer assistants. It is well to provide these with some special badge or insignia and give them special privileges.[46]

This was, of course, part of the development of a colonial administration (subjects selected from the ranks of the oppressed by the oppressor and elevated to a managerial/custodial position in the social structure) among the colonized children.* But it was also a seemingly logical

---

*This same practice was employed by the New York City Parks Department in organizing its Auxiliary Park Police, mentioned in Chapter 3.

strategy of organization which served two additional purposes beyond the creation of an elite native crust. First,
often the boys who were picked as strongest and given priv-
ileges were the same male "gang members" that the playground feared most as a threat to stability. On the Lower
East Side, these boys were bought off with jobs as playground assistants,[47] and so a pattern of buying off dissi-
dents which had come to the fore in adult society through
business unionism had its counterpart and training camp
for future labor leaders in the workings of the playground.
Second, the creation of a hierarchical, organizational
framework, with privilege based on that hierarchy, was
now legitimized as a universal form of social intercourse
for the child. In school, at work, and now on the
playground, social relations were governed by a vertical
division of labor and rewards. Power was thus maintained
by mediating the perceptions of the children. They could
not see the Lees or Schiffs or Carnegies who were the real
powers in control of the finances; they rarely saw the
Gulicks or Weirs or Hetheringtons who were the techno-
cratic originators of playground organization; and with the
creation of an assistant corps (whether composed of gang
members or Boy Scouts), their access to the one adult with
whom they did have daily contact and who did have a
semblance of power was now made more difficult. Ben
Levine remembers thinking of the Boy Scouts as the
"aristocracy of the playground."[48] This conception reveals
the degree to which the class element of the playground
had been successfully blunted, as the Boy Scouts were
hardly "aristocracy" but must have been perceived as such
since they often organized the teams, controlled access to
equipment, and generally were responsible for what
seemed to be the major decisions governing everyday life
on the playground. Subsequently, we can see that, as in the
world of work, where Marglin[49] and others have shown that
hierarchy was used as a tool of alienation, the same process
was occurring on the playground. Organization meant
obfuscation and that translated into a feeling of powerlessness and frustration. Perhaps the fact that in some cities
children only remained on the playground for an average of
a half hour can be traced to this anxiety of powerlessness.

In addition to the organization of assistant corps, "The Normal Course of Play" called for: enrollment and the taking of attendance twice daily (even though it was time-consuming, it was worthwhile as a discipline aid); closing and opening exercises such as flag salutes and marching drills ("usually popular with the girls and unpopular with the boys"); a strict control of supplies ("should be kept under lock and key"); tournaments and teams.[50] Each technique taught discipline, property rights, and a worship of commodities. Each technique was a quantitative move toward consolidation of power by the reformers which eventually established a qualitatively new kind of leisure world for the children and workers. Opening exercises, for example, were rituals that served as lines of demarcation, boundaries separating the time and space of free play from play which was directed/supervised/controlled. It was a daily initiation rite. Teams were not only models of cooperation (set in an overall framework of competition), but also an education in property rights. As "The Normal Course" put it:

> Every child on the playground should be organized into as many different teams as possible. They become responsible for property.[51]

Tournaments were valued as publicity, as ways of interesting parents, and also as exercises in consumerism. Despite much propaganda about eliminating prizes which had worth in themselves and substituting medals or badges or trophies that were only of symbolic value, as late as 1912 track meets sponsored by the Parks and Playground Association of the City of New York were offering prizes of "a small camera, a pair of skates, several games, books, and a number of small articles." Nationally, in "113 out of 127 national playgrounds surveyed respondents offered prizes for competitions."[52] Can anyone begin to assess the psychological impact of such rewards on the minds of Jewish and other immigrant children whose every other waking hour was a lesson in mere survival? Is it any surprise then that the report of the New York Parks and Playgrounds Association notes that all these prizes which also included movie tickets "were greatly appreciated"?[53] Is it any question who

and what would be on the receiving end of such appreciation? The appreciation by the winners of course meant that
there was resentment and disgruntlement by the losers.
Often the children had to be instructed not to "dispute
decisions, cheer opponent's mistakes," and the like. Rewards and tournaments were tricky things for the reformers as there were always more losers than winners, and thus
potentially more dissatisfied children than appreciative
ones. Indeed, when speaking about the conduct of a
tournament, "The Normal Course" insisted that "The
attendance of one or more policemen should be secured"—
to help keep back the crowd and to "quell disorder if any
should arise."[54] All the newspaper accounts and publicity
pictures of the early tournaments at Seward Park, Hamilton
Fish Park, and others in New York, verify the playground
directors' reliance on police. The process of building
hegemony and developing false consciousness takes time.
The elite, recognizing this, set out to control whomever
they could in whatever way they could, until such
ideological rooting could take hold. If police were needed,
police were used. If prohibitions against "smoking, swearing, yelling, using insulting language, disobedience, obscenity, destructiveness, stealing and improper conduct"[55]
worked to discourage a challenge to established norms—
the children fearing disqualification in the race for prizes
or notices sent to the children's court—these techniques
were deployed. Pure pragmatism reduced all ends to means
as power was sought and the children were caught.

By 1910, *The Playground* was reporting that 246 cities
had established supervised playgrounds for the first time in
the last two years. "The Normal Course of Play" had been
adopted for use in twenty-one educational institutions,[56]
among them New York University (where Curtis taught),
Harvard (where Joseph Lee's money provided a position for
George Johnson), Columbia, and other elite universities.[57]
With the financial assistance of a grant of $5,000 per year,
Clark Hetherington traveled to 300 cities in thirty-five
states over the years 1909-12, promoting the findings and
philosophies of "The Normal Course" and the Playground
Association of America. The play movement was growing

swiftly as a national, and particularly urban, phenomenon. As a case in point, between the years 1905 and 1910 New York City more than doubled the number of publicly maintained playgrounds. In 1910 New York City spent $121,606 for playground maintenance, employing 949 workers at over 250 playground sites.[58] Seventy-eight cities had playground associations, and the progressive as well as conservative press was filled with glowing accounts of happy, contented children and endorsements of the play movement from people at both ends of the political spectrum.

The Playground Association of America, as both cause and effect of this trend, employed nine field secretaries by the middle of 1913 and thirteen by the end of that year.[59] It took seriously its self-appointed mission of pitching the ideas, and shaping and guiding the playground movement, believing that play "contains the beginnings of all subsequent development and culture."[60] With that kind of prize in the air, the PAA concentrated on the ground. In 1906, the association had been organized "with a negative idea— to keep children off the streets."[61] By the second decade of the century, it had more positive goals in mind—socialization for family life, for citizenship, and for production.

PART TWO **The Decline of
Jewish Immigrant
Street Life**

Introduction

If the first four chapters of this book have documented the rise of organized play, then the next four will catalogue the decline of immigrant Jewish street life and culture. The first four chapters imply the concluding four. The successes of people like Jacob Riis, Luther Gulick, and Joseph Lee were contingent on the failure of the immigrants to root, maintain, and expand their cultural forms in the New World or under new conditions.

The playgrounds, the vacation schools, and the settlement houses pushed and pulled at the threads of the immigrants' social fabric. Children and adults alike were confused by the attention paid their activities. Many knew how to defend themselves against the approaches of Christian missionaries, labor scabs, and hostile police, but the wiles of playground directors who offered free cameras as prizes for playing their games, their way...well, that was another matter. Playing on the playground provided youngsters with a chance to gain notoriety in the press; to receive rewards like books, movie tickets, and trophies; and to avoid arrest by cops enforcing the antistreet-play laws. Slowly but surely, the immigrants' community of play began to crumble.

Part of the collapse of immigrant street culture can be

understood as a movement from God to games. These Jewish immigrants emerged from the *shtetln* and towns of Eastern Europe with a religious-centered sense of time, but in the New World time was rationalized to conform to the machine. The organized-play movement played an extremely important role in socializing tens of thousands of children in such a way as to fit them for this new rational temporality. The Sabbath was secularized and activities such as work, leisure, prayer, and play were compartmentalized to conform with the new American ethos.

Another theme that emerges from the collapse of immigrant street life is the theme of sexuality as mixed with sport and suppression. Since the rise of corporate capitalism, women have essentially been locked out of the ballpark, sports becoming what one social critic has called "a male soap opera." As a result, women have suffered physiologically, socially, and psychologically. By studying the attitudes held and the programs developed by the leaders of the organized-play movement concerning women, we get a good sense of how and why the sex-role socialization of the modern era came to be. We can also learn how the ideology of excluding women from sports influenced and was influenced by male notions of sexuality, family, and child-rearing. Both sex and sport turn around the axis of the body, and so we will examine the mind–body splits of Taylorism, the mystification which surrounded the body as a result of Victorian morality, and issues such as procreation, birth control, and "sex tension."

In addition to the issues of time and space and sexuality and sport, there emerges from our study of the rise of organized play and the decline of immigrant culture the problem of work. As we have seen, the nature of play was strongly shaped by the nature of work in an industrializing America. Children on the Lower East Side and elsewhere were to be trained on the playgrounds and in the vacation schools to their future stations as hard-working members of the laboring class, and they were to be schooled in an understanding of what labor in America was all about— property. Playgrounds were to play an important role in combatting juvenile delinquency and in teaching immigrant and working-class youth to respect and obey "the rules of the game," whether the game be basketball or capitalism.

The chapters that follow examine the above themes with one eye toward the destruction of the immigrant street life of East European Jews on the Lower East Side of New York. The other eye will be focused on the implications of the rise of organized play on other sectors of the working class and in other sections of the country.

It is not inequality of wealth or political oppression as direct causes which have wrecked the great nations....Nations have blossomed or perished according to the use they made of the leisure time of the people.

—John Collier
People's Institute of New York

CHAPTER 5 **Time and Space:
An Afternoon Down and
Fifty Years to Pay**

When the Jews of the *shtetl* emigrated to America at the
turn of the century, time became a matter of power rather
than piety. In the *shtetl* time had been regulated by nature
and God. Nature was manifest in the requirements of car-
ing for animals, firing a furnace, and all the task orien-
tations of a preindustrial economy. The ordering of
personal and communal life was also informed by God—
structured as prayer, ritual, and holiday. The Sabbath was
"a foretaste of the future,"[1] a world free of worry, suffused
with joy, and colored with a messianic hope for humankind.
The otherwise commonplace of everyday life was wrapped
in a religious shroud (talis) which even if tattered by the
forces of enlightenment (Haskalah) and persecution was
nevertheless a garment that brought sequence, substance,
and transcendence to the Jews of Eastern Europe. However,
with the arrival of capitalism or the departure of Jews to an
industrializing America, the nature of time changed.

The familiar rhythms of religious services, chores, and
the Sabbath were replaced by the relentless pace of the
process of capital accumulation. Time became currency to
be spent by the worker and bought by the boss, rather than
something to be passed.[2] Time was no longer signaled by
the sound of the crow or the call to *shul* by the setting sun.
It was different, as Harry Roskolenko remembers:

87

Time was the rasping foreman's voice echoing the foreman's own needs. It had neither a moon nor a sun nor heroes.[3]

The metamorphosis of time from a personal-communal to an abstract phenomenon involved several adjustments which were part adaptation and part coercion. Adjustments were necessary within days—the development of work and leisure time; within weeks—the creation of weekends as extensions of rather than refutations of the work week; and within life spans—childhood as a time for play, maturity as conformity to alienation. Each adjustment created, and in turn was created by, a corresponding nonwork institution which served to soften and institutionalize the changes. For nonwork, prework, or after-work time there was the park, the playground, and finally, the evening recreation center; for weekends, lectures, dances, and excursions to the outer boroughs. Lastly, for the "mature adult" there was the institution of childhood which one could experience vicariously through the leisure of children or the spectacle of professional games. The development of each of these institutions involved a simultaneous regression of immigrant processes and institutions. The desecration and desanctification of the Sabbath, the disembowelment of May Day, and the destruction of the integrated nature of autonomous street play all evolved from the adjustment of time to capitalist rationality. With the commoditization of time under a capitalist-positivist ethos nothing remained "outside," for "outsideness," as social philosopher Max Horkheimer put it, is the very source of fear. Everyone and everything was subsumed under the ever-sweeping, ever-moving hands of the clock which alternately pushed and pulled a society into the modern era—and the Jewish working class into conformity.

From God to Games

The secularization of leisure proceeded apace with the destruction of religious-natural time as the way of ordering work and communal functions. With the weakening of religious ties as a result of proletarianization, the belief systems of many Jews were left in limbo. They required new interpretation and new forms. In the United States, education played the primary role in developing a belief system and a world view, but there was also a substantial segment of the population (and segments of those who believed in education) that "renewed its faith" through Socialism and/or sport.

Although the number of Jews who constituted "fans" at various sports events is impossible to calculate, we do have indication that they were significantly interested in the doings of sports. One indication was the rise of Jewish sports heroes. When, for example, Benjamin Kauff (nicknamed the "Ty Cobb of the Feds") played for the New York Yankees in 1912, he "was such a magnet at the gate that New York Giant manager cast covetous eyes at him."[4] Howe notes that "Jewish boys became fanatics of baseball, their badge as Americans."[5] Yet another indication of the involvement of Jews with sports can be found in the records of the Yiddish press, which by 1908 was forced to carry boxing results—no doubt to allow greater appreciation of the likes of Joe ("The Pride of the Ghetto") Bernstein, Abe ("The Little Hebrew") Attell, and others.[6] Even as early as 1903, the Jews' devotion to sports merited a thousand-word editorial by *Forward* editor Abe Cahan, which read in part:

> A father writes a letter about baseball and asks our advice. He sees baseball as a foolish and wild game. But, his boy, who is already in the higher classes of the school register, is himself eager to play. The view which the father expresses is not only his. The majority of our immigrant parents have such an opinion about this matter.
>
> ..."Here in the gorgeous America, big people play baseball. They run around after a piece of suede and fight with themselves because of this like small boys," the father writes! "I believe a boy should grow to be a man not a wild American runner."
>
> [Cahan answers:] Let your boy play baseball and become excellent in playing the game. It should not interfere with their studies and they should not become dragged down in bad company...[but] why shouldn't you let him go?
>
> In a healthy body lives a healthy mind. In a quick body a quick wisdom. Mainly, let us not so raise the children that they should grow up foreigners in their own birthplace.[7]

If they were not to "grow up foreigners" in the land of America, Jews were going to have to acquiesce to the desanctification of the Sabbath and transform it from a day of prayer and synagogue to a day of play and playground. In 1891, when twenty-seven rabbis preached sermons for parks and playgrounds in New York City[8] as part of the reformers' campaign for play space, they could not foresee that a decade later their prayers would be answered paradoxically with the opening of Seward Park and Hamilton Fish Park on Saturdays. But the shift from God to games was engulfing all leisure time in the urban arena, Jewish and non-Jewish alike. The first crack in the Sabbath shell came in 1894 with an attempt by Brooklyn Judge (and later Mayor) William Gaynor to allow "quietly played baseball in the new wards"[9] and although it took a full eighty years to eliminate the final vestiges of religious proscription of Sabbath sports participation (the ban on Sunday horse racing in New York State was lifted in 1974), the secularization of time through leisure at the turn of the century played a critical role in the molding of the immigrant working class.

In 1893, the New York Court of Appeals in *People v. Moses* upheld the conviction of a defendant prosecuted for fishing on Sunday. Its decision stated in part that "The Christian Sabbath is one of the civil institutions of the State." The state, according to the court, had the responsibility for guiding the moral, physical, and mental well-being of the people, and fishing on the Sabbath was a challenge to that protection. Its citing of another case to add the weight of precedent reveals much about the legal tenor of the times:

> That playing ball by several persons in a place open to the view of the people in the vicinity, or who may pass by is condemned by the principles which lie at the bottom of the Sunday laws...[10]

But while decisions seesawed back and forth regarding the propriety of play on the Sabbath (Sections 259 and 265 of the New York State Penal Code), the dynamics of an ever-increasing mechanization coupled with a militant working-class movement that demanded the reduction of hours in the work week made Sabbath play an inevitability. In the garment trade, for example, from 1884 to 1904 the length of the average work week shrank as follows:[11]

Task	1884 (hrs)	1896 (hrs)	1904 (hrs)
Cutter	55–58.5	54	48–52
Cloakmaker	84	72	59
Presser	84	n.a.	56

It is true, as Philip Foner notes in his *History of the Labor Movement in the United States,* that "All over the United States long working hours were the rule."[12] But the times, they were achangin'.

The eight-hour-day movement was "everywhere," according to *John Swinton's Paper* in mid-April 1886.[13] By that time there were approximately 250,000 industrial workers involved, and 30,000 of them had already been granted a nine- or eight-hour day. Workers smoked "Eight-Hour Tobacco," wore "Eight-Hour Shoes," and articulated their demands for temporal-cultural emancipation in an "Eight-Hour Song":

> We mean to make things over; we're tired to toil for
> naught
> But bare enough to live on: never an hour for thought.
> We want to feel the sunshine; we want to smell the
> flowers;
> We're sure that God has willed it, and we mean to have
> eight hours.[14]

As a result of all the eight-hour agitation and the strikes held on May 1, 1886, "it was estimated that 185,000 out of 350,000 workers who struck for the eight-hour day gained their demand on May 1 and the days following."[15] Thousands more had their hours reduced.

From the start, the mass movement for the eight-hour day evoked fear and trembling from the upper class, who denounced it as "Communism, lurid and rampant," and who believed that it would encourage "loafing and gambling, rioting, debauchery and drunkenness."[16] For this class there was a twofold problem. First, the movement for decreased work time led by the unions, and later by the Socialist party, meant that there would be an increased possibility of the development of an autonomous working-class culture (like the one which had evolved on the streets of the Lower East Side) linked to a revolutionary or progressive political movement. This was, of course, anathema. And second, the demographics of immigration and an expanding population meant that vast numbers of children would be free to roam the streets in preschool or nonschool time, developing individual and mass psychologies which could countervail the time–work discipline demanded by industrial capitalism.[17] Thus, playground psychologist G. Stanley Hall warned in 1904 that "everything in conduct should be mechanized as early and completely as possible"[18] as a way of adjusting to the demands of the age. An article in *The Playground* by John Collier a few years later took both the child and the time-emancipated adult into consideration. Collier wrote that the problem of the twentieth century was "not the distribution of wealth or conservation of natural resources, but rather the utilization of the leisure time of the people." He offered, ". . . nations have blossomed or perished according to the use they made of the leisure time of the people."[19] An opiate for the masses was needed to supplement or replace a waning religion. Secular sports, which could inculcate a sense of time discipline in youth and safely occupy the leisure time of workers, all under the waving American flag, was therefore duly enshrined. The Jewish Sabbath fell first, but the Christian Sabbath would follow.

In 1904, there were test cases in no less than three professional ballparks in the metropolitan area on one day, as justices and entrepreneurs alike smashed at the hallowed "day of rest." In Brooklyn, a crowd of 13,000 jeered as the police arrested the pitcher, batter, catcher, and three program/ticket-sellers at one game. Four days later they were discharged because there was "no evidence of any violation."[20] Although the organized-play leaders argued against professional sports on Sunday, patricianly describing them as work and therefore not worthy of exemption from Sunday Blue Laws, their arguments fitted and their cause was partially served by professional sports on Sunday. In 1910, Joseph Lee, then president of the Playground Association of America, delivered a speech entitled "Sunday Play" at the Fourth Annual Recreation Congress of the

PAA. In it, he argued that "Sunday laws forbidding play and sport are in the main an evil." "Sunday," he said, was to be "the day of fulfillment to those essential purposes of life for which the weekday has left no room." He cited a young man who "spent the week bending over the columns of a ledger" and a young woman who "has passed the working days standing at a machine making a few simple motions of the hand," and asserted that special compensation was needed. Play would thus supplement the "great industrial principle and chief means of modern civilization"—specialization. In "preparing the man for his employment and modifying the employment to fit the man," Lee held that Sunday play was vitally important in order "to provide" room for that part of each man's life which his daily industry has shown itself unable to contain.[21]

In order to compensate for the life-crippling week suffered by the workers, Lee and his teammates would recreate the Sabbath. The reformers sponsored dance halls, concerts, lectures, outings, and the like, all as part of the movement for Sunday play. These events, when combined with the lure of professional sports, social clubs, lodges, politically sponsored picnics, and balls, meant a secularization of the Sabbath. Against this large-scale assault, God never really had a chance.

May Day

> I felt like I was involved in something beyond my immediate interest. The first of May I worked in a shop. . . . I felt a sense of consciousness and obligation. . . . I didn't care if I'd be fired. . . . "I am a class-conscious worker; the First of May is a workers' holiday." I did it even if I had to lose half a day's wages and jeopardize my job. I did it time and again.[22]

If the desecration of the Sabbath and its subsequent colonization through leisure by the upper class was a substantial step in transforming "free" time from an institution of freedom to one of alienation for the working class, then the destruction of holidays was another. From May 1, 1886, on, May Day was considered by thousands a workers' holiday, a time to show class consciousness and international solidarity. In New York City, close to 25,000 people marched in a torchlight parade down Broadway and into Union Square. In Detroit, 11,000 marched; in Chicago, 40,000 workers struck and not a train moved while "most of the industries in Chicago were paralyzed." None of this sat well with the elite and so they immediately began a counteroffensive of Pinkerton and police attacks, conspiracy charges, injunctions, and the like. In New York City alone, the iron fist resulted in "legal roundups" of more than 100 people on conspiracy charges in two months of 1886. Ultimately, the outrages of the police led to the formation of labor parties and workers' support for the 1886 campaign of Henry George against the redbaiting organized-play leader and iron magnate Abraham Hewitt.[23] But all this, and the subsequent intricacies of New York City (or national) labor and Labor party politics, is beyond our scope. We mention it here only as a reminder that there are two sides to the Americanization of immigrants and the socialization of workers—coercion and adaptation.

Adaptation came in the form of settlement house-, playground-, and PAA-sponsored programs celebrating Washington's, Lincoln's and Christ's birthdays, as well as St. Valentine's Day. These settlement programs or playground activities diverted workers from an identification with class-based holidays like May Day which had helped to sustain a culture of struggle within the working class. A blunt and scathing article in a Socialist paper, *The Worker*, appeared on May 1, 1903, addressed to such diversions:

THE ABSURDITY OF PERSONAL HOLIDAYS
Let the capitalist state decree the celebration of personal holidays in honor of great men who are popularly supposed to have determined the course of history in their private persons, and to whom is given the credit for an age of the nation's collective effort; we choose rather to celebrate the collective spirit of the race as expressed in its most vital class, the collective aspirations and effort, the social movement of our time.

When we lose our superstitions about great men and the individualistic illusions of hero worship; when society becomes sane and not so morbidly modest, it will celebrate itself. . . . [24]

Not only were there settlement-sponsored holiday cele-
brations and citywide festivities such as the Fulton–Hud-
son gala of 1909, but there were the more direct intentions
of the various immigrant restriction leagues,[25] many of
whose members were organized-play leaders of long standing. The North American Civic League, founded by the
YMCA in 1907, was one such organization set on restrict-
ing the influx of immigrants and on the inculcation of
proper American customs and virtues for those already
arrived. "Composed by and large of representatives of the
more conservative economic interests," the NACL set out
to "educate the immigrant workers"[26] who "were frequently
brought under the influence of 'mischievous radicals.'"[27]
The league's intent was to "lessen the danger of industrial
disorders and economic unrest."[28] Its program included
sending "teachers" into the factories and shops of major
immigration cities (New York included) at noon and mid-
night and organizing the immigrants into classes for learning English, American history, and civics. It also included
distributing "Messages to Newcomers to the United States"
which informed the immigrant in his/her native tongue
about American law, customs, and Abe Lincoln.[29] Last but
not least, the NACL was involved in recreation, for it
"believed that wholesome recreation was essential to
sound teaching."[30] Thus, the league took very seriously
Bella Mead's observation that "In the attempt to accomplish [a homogeneous civilization], the line of least resistance will be found on the side of amusements and
pleasures."[31]

With the holidays—the presidential birthdays, the Independence or Founder's days, Christmas, etc.—was born the
festival of the modern era. But these were festivals unlike
those known to the Jews of the *shtetl* where marriages were
contracted, exuberance reigned, and the scarcity of poverty
was suspended and superseded by music, myth, mirth, and
magic. These were festivals unlike the May Day parades
where "people dressed in their best"[32] and the streets of toil
were transformed into spaces of liberation, where the
remorseless face of the clock was blocked by the shadows
cast by thousands of class-conscious workers and their
families. These festivals were merely ornaments that

adorned everyday life, emotional fetters which helped to
extend domination and curtail transformation. These were
festivals of unwanted fate and unfilled fantasy.

Night and Day

As the Sabbath was secularized and as holidays were
shaped to conform to the elite's needs, so too were the after-
work hours. Although there were still long and hard hours
of work in the sweatshops, and although the irregularity of
the "slack season" still made for periods of completely
empty days, by the start of the second decade of the 1900s
one could discern a fairly regular pattern to most workers'
lives. Charles Stein was typical. He rose at six in the morning, left the house where he boarded, and headed either for
the public showers (twice a week) or went directly to a
cafeteria where he read the papers. After a ten-cent break-
fast consisting of coffee and two rolls, he headed off for
work which began promptly at 7:30, but for which he had to
arrive by 7:15. Work lasted until noon when there was a
half-hour lunch break, followed by an additional five and a
half or six hours of work. After work he ate and then either
proceeded to night school, did homework, went to the
cafes, read Socialist or union literature, or went to lectures,
meetings, or union affairs.[33] On certain days there were
demonstrations or a visit to the Yiddish theater or the Met.
Similarly, many workers substituted nights at home with
the family or friends or (if young) nights at dance halls,
parks, promenading, tending house, or on the roofs where,
as "theoreticians of the roofs,"[34] they discussed politics and
sang Russian folksongs while perched high above the
sweatshops that oppressed them. Stein summed up what
should be obvious: "The problem was not what to do with
your time...."

However, what was not a problem for the working class
became one for the elite, and so an increased emphasis was
placed on the role of the evening recreation center. Shorter
hours of work meant more time for leisure and this was
threatening to employers in their quest for ever-greater
profits. As historian Jesse Pope points out, "No employer

would think of reducing the working time of his employees until requested to do so by the entire body of workmen."[35] And a simple "request" was hardly enough. Strikes and the threat of strikes were the key tools of the working class in the struggle for the reduction of the workday.

But there were other fears that the elite had concerning leisure time. A Department of Education report on playgrounds and evening recreation centers focused on another worry:

> The great problem confronting the recreation center principal and teachers is the filling of the leisure time of the working men and women with a combination of recreation and athletic activities which will help make their lives more tolerable.[36]

Making their lives more tolerable did not mean correcting the injustice and exploitation of the shops, it merely meant providing a program of more instant gratification under the supervision and control of the reformers. Workers were unaccustomed to waiting until the Sabbath or a holiday to partake of recreation, and so the reformers decided to adjust the structure of their programs. Hence, the evening recreation center burst onto the leisure scene.

Although evening recreation centers had been a part of the municipal organized-play structure since 1900, they were always second cousins to playgrounds and vacation schools. This reflected a conscious decision by the elite to concentrate its efforts on children. That concentration was not abandoned, but it is significant to note that during the period 1909–14 in New York City, the number of vacation schools alternately increased and decreased, finally advancing in numbers from thirty to thirty-six. During that same period, playground growth took giant leaps and then suffered cutbacks, plummeting from 246 in 1909 to 116 in 1910, and then surging to 236 in 1911 before dropping to 197 in 1914. While all this was happening, evening recreation centers were growing by more than 250 percent, and there was not one year in which their numbers did not increase.[37] In raw numbers, the evening recreation centers went from twenty-two to thirty-two, to forty-eight, to fifty-six, to sixty-two centers over the years 1909–14. Superintendent of Schools William Maxwell, a frequent contributor to *The Playground* and a lecturer on his respect for play as an "Americanizing" tool, captured the significance of the increase in political and mathematical terms. He wrote in the Department of Education's (1911–1912) Fourteenth Annual Playground Report:

> The working classes will have additional time on their hands after their labors for the days are finished [because of the impending law which was to limit factory employment to 54 hours per week for men and women under 18]. The work of the recreation center becomes a special and redoubled interest.[38]

The evening recreation center became part of the reformers' campaign for a "Wider Use of the School Plant."[39] The centers consisted of game rooms, music rooms, gym classes, apparatus work and gymnastics, prizes for marathons, study rooms, drama groups, and clubs.[40] Some held classes in etiquette or how to apply for a job, and maintained employment registers toward that end.[41] They ran from 7:00 P.M. until 10:00 or 11:00, covering the time that the propertied class feared most. Lee Hanmer put it squarely concerning the nocturnal hours: "In that most dangerous time of all the day, from six to eleven P.M., occur eighty percent of all the offenses against society."[42]

Given the rise in influence and power of the Socialist party, and given the economic depression of 1913, the reformers were caught in a bind to develop an instant-gratification leisure-time program that would "develop a type" that was a "credit to our civilization."[43] In 1912, Socialist party membership reached its height of 118,000 and the Socialist press published a total of 323 English- and foreign-language daily, weekly, and monthly papers/journals/magazines. Mabel Dodge was hosting salon teas where Wobblies, Socialists, and anarchists would come and hold forth about the respective merits of each ideology.[44] Professor Charles Beard noted that early twentieth-century Socialism was "admittedly shaking the old foundations of politics the world over and penetrating our science, art and literature."[45] He neglected to mention that within the political arena over 300 Socialists held municipal, state, and congressional positions.[46]

In New York City, Socialist-led unions held mass strikes that involved tens of thousands of people, and street-corner rallies, announced in the pages of the *Forward* and the *Call*, were held almost nightly with crowds of upward of a few hundred gathered around each speaker. Ultimately, the Socialist strength in New York was revealed as 21.7 percent of the mayoral vote went to the Socialist party candidate in the 1917 election, Morris Hillquit, the former rooftop theoretician.[47] The dialectics of a Socialist rise and an economic decline put the elite on the defense. The evening recreation centers, consciously geared toward heading off the further encroachment of Socialism, were evoked with the hope that a good offense is the best defense.

Day and Night

The Evening recreation centers never really caught on. They were unpopular with the immigrants and the military preparations for World War I usurped most of the time and efforts of municipal government. But other attempts to structure the recreation of children and adolescents continued, in line with the time and space elements of the factory system. In fact, it is impossible to really understand the phenomenology of the playground without analyzing everyday life in the sweatshop and the philosophy of Taylorism which prevailed there.

In his excellent study of scientific management in the Progressive Era, historian Samuel Haber writes:

> The factory for Taylor was not only an instrument for the production of goods and profits, it was also a moral gymnasium for the exercise of character.[48]

Indeed, just as play is composed of situations which alternately accept and challenge both time and space, so too is the modern factory an arena wherein time and space are approached dialectically. To the child engaged in play where he or she controls the goals, pace, and process, play is liberatory and time is opportunity. A child engaged by a coach, settlement house, or club is a mere representative, and with the process out of the child's control, time is an obstacle. Similarly with space and the worker: when the worker controls what–how–when–if things get produced, time and space are elements in the worker's development as a conscious being. When production is alienated, time becomes pain and space the plane of suffering. Taylorism, although described by its advocates as "physical efficiency," contributed significantly to alienation in the factory, the Socialists describing it as "a refined form of exploitation."[49] In the sweatshop, however, the "refinement" was hard to locate.

Time in the sweatshop was a matter of intensity for the worker and evasion for the bosses. The ten-, twelve-, and sometimes sixteen-hour days were stretches of intense concentration and oppression for the sweaters. Time was everywhere and weighed heavily on the bodies and souls of the immigrants as this heart-rending poem of Morris Rosenfeld, himself a worker in the shops, portrays:

IN THE SHOP
The clock in the workshop—it rests not a moment!
It points on, and ticks on; eternity—time;
And once someone told me the clock had a meaning—
Its pointing and ticking had reason and rhyme.
And this too he told me, or had I been dreaming—
The clock wakened life in one forces unseen,
And something besides;. . . I forget what, O ask not!
I know not, I know not, I am a machine.

At times, when I listen, I hear the clock plainly;
The reason of old—the old meaning is gone!
The maddening pendulum urges me forward
To labor and still labor on.
The tick of the clock is the boss in his anger!
The face of the clock has the eyes of the foe;
The clock—O I shudder—Dost hear how it draws me?
It calls me "Machine" and it cries to me "Sew!"[50]

During the Progressive Era, labor laws were subject to differing interpretations, lax enforcement, graft, and inadequate staffing of factory and store inspectors. Knowing this, and knowing that in a job-related accident the burden of proof was on the employee to show negligence, workers had to be extremely intense about their work lest they become disabled with no benefits.[51] While it is true that elite organizations like the National Civic Federation (NCF) were drafting and passing more liberal workmen's compensation laws, these went only so far as was necessary to blunt more radical proposals put forth by leftists for industrial democracy. Utilities magnate Samuel Insull spoke to the workers' compensation bills, minimum-wage bills, and regulation of public utilities—all of which were drafted by the NCF around 1910. He said that he preferred to "help shape the right kind of legislation [before] the wrong kind [was] forced upon him."[52]

What was forced on the workers was much more severe in its impact than the potential curtailment of profits so feared by Insull, the NCF, the National Association of Manufacturers, and members of the capitalist class, both large and small. Time in the sweatshops of the Lower East Side meant fines for broken thread or damaged garments, low wages that barely kept pace with cost of living increases, a bad-odds bet against injury from accidents and fire, and perpetual motion. Workers were usually required to furnish their own sewing machines, and operators were fined ten cents or twenty-five cents for damaging "the goods."[53] Despite tremendous growth in production between the years 1897 and 1915, real wages remained stationary, with price rises swallowing up gains in money income: "Studies of living standards among unskilled workers in New York City indicated that wages were at subsistence levels or below."[54] The Triangle Fire of March 1911, which took the lives of 146 workers, symbolized the Russian-roulette-like nature of time spent in firetrap buildings.[55] All this was "time" for the workers—time "spent" frantically as Harry Roskolenko relates about his father:

> His small body was like a piece of sculpture caught in some form of motion; an engine puffing; an engine riding into a station; a bursting continuity of steam, thin muscles, sharp reflexes—and cloak went after cloak, done, counted. On and on it went, wearing him to death.[56]

This time of intensity for the workers during which they

became "a sort of living automatic part of a machine"[57] was a time of evasion for the bosses. Time robbed the bosses of their opportunity to accumulate more capital and profits when the length of the working day was regulated; when it limited the availability of children by age; and when it pushed them to keep up with their competitors. The first intrusion of time was often dealt with by stealth; many bosses covered the face of the clock, setting it back during worktime and ahead during lunch, arbitrarily withholding agreed-upon wages and pay schedules. The second intrusion was circumvented by paying older siblings for work done by underage children who, because of the infrequency of factory inspections could be found "hangin' around" almost every factory, working and stopping according to the announced arrival of the inspector.[58] The last factor, fierce competition, endemic to the garment industry in particular because of the low level of capitalization needed to become a contractor,[59] meant the introduction of any and all time-saving devices regardless of their effects on the human beings forced to adapt them. The long-cutting knife which could prepare material for assembly much quicker than earlier cutting methods, but which was also heavier in weight, replaced women cutters.[60] The team system similarly displaced the skilled tailor, and had an adverse effect on union organizing and skill development.[61] No matter to the bosses—factories, as Abraham Cahan's immigrant novel *David Levinsky* shows us, were the new temples for the propertied class where homage was paid to the god Time and his sister Profits.[62] The result was nothing short of catastrophic—rhythmless days of tedium, tension, and trial.

This lack of rhythm carried over into the playground where only music chosen from an approved list of songs was allowed to be played. Ragtime music, which revealed and reflected the tempo of the age in a series of notes, scores, and refrains that burst into the collective ear and were just as soon replaced by the next set of notes and bars, was banned.[63] Ragtime communicated a perhaps too-accurate sense of massing, moving America. It cut too near the nerve of industrial capitalism, bringing to the playground a frenzy and looseness that made the reformers uncomfortable. But although ragtime was banned because it cut too close to capitalism's nerve, the clock, which was part of that nerve fiber, was not. Rose Fortune, a garment worker who wrote eloquently about her experiences and evocatively of her exploitation, noted that the clock was hated because at the end of a too-long day "The remorseless clock informed us that there were two hours more of this torture...."[64] This same clock—an agent of pain, a symbol of compulsion—was nevertheless a highly significant piece of playground equipment. As an inanimate representative of Taylorism and exploitation, it came to perform three crucial functions: first, the clock separated the time of leisure from the time of work, the playground time from school or factory time; second, the clock worked to compartmentalize experiences on the playground itself; last, the clock became a measure of success and a device for realizing hierarchy within the play sphere. The three functions overlapped and intertwined to inform the nonwork world of the inevitable necessity of punctuality, periodicity, and performance.

Punctuality

"The Normal Course of Play" put the matter succinctly and in its most absurd form. Writing about the conduct of tournaments held on playgrounds, it advised potential playground directors: "Every event should be begun on time whether the children are there or not."[65] The mind boggles at the degree of abstraction that must have been attained in order seriously to consider this imposition of form without content. In the great morality play being enacted, the children were at best second-string performers. If, having been given a chance to participate, they muffed it, points were to be deducted (for lateness as well as improper conduct). Just as factory workers like Charles Stein were forced to arrive at their jobs a quarter of an hour early to avoid being docked pay or even fired, so too were the children commanded to be punctual. Even in nontournament situations, the children were to be assembled in one spot by the designated hour and then a flag raising, salute, pledge, and perhaps some marching or a talk by the supervisor[66] would ensue, thus formally separating the time of play from the time of work. Given the oppressive nature of the factory or sweatshop, such a separation has its positive aspects, but the formalized division also negatively serves to isolate and limit play. Play as social intercourse is atomized and work becomes ever more repressive.

Periodicity

Recurrence and periodicity, when added to the demand for punctuality, compose a setting of boredom built on coercion. As in the workaday world of corporate society, the clock's regularity and divisiveness comes to take on a generative quality. Thus, what historian E. P. Thompson calls the "familiar landscape of industrial capitalism," which included "the timesheet [and] the time-keeper,"[67] imposed itself on the playground structure as well. The field staff of the New York City Recreation Bureau, for example, probably taking its lead from the field secretaries of the Playground Association of America, inspected playgrounds and verified time reports, utilized time sheets, etc. Even more serious was the division of the playground day into segments, the artificial character of which could not be lost to anyone familiar with the flow and continuity of autonomous street play. The typical New York City vacation playground day was segmented/organized as follows:[68]

1:00–1:30	—assembly (marching, singing, flag salutes, talk by principal
1:30–2:30	—organized games (kindergarten, gymnasium)
2:30–3:00	—organized free play
3:00–4:00	—drills, folk dancing, apparatus work, occupational work
4:00–4:45	—organized games, basketball (gymnastics, kindergarten)
4:45–5:15	—athletics, good citizens club
5:15–5:30	—dismissal (singing and marching)

This systematic preplanning and precalculation of experience had its birth in the scientific management of Taylor, and reflected at least partially the concerns of people like

Lee and G. S. Hall, who thought that the monotony of modern industry "needs to be offset by compensating modes of activity."[69] "Order" was seen as "the condition of time possession";[70] and in the dual-pronged struggle with anarchy and overindustrialization, a schedule was developed which had the purpose of creating order (combatting chaos) while allowing for freedom of choice (combatting monotony). The playground would demand compliance with the broader framework of ordering and then allow "free choice" within the established parameters. A child could, between the half hour from 2:30 until 3:00, for example, indulge in prisoner's base, tag, or other accepted games—so long as he or she was willing to commence and terminate at the correct time. Thus, compulsion was mitigated by a sense of freedom, and perhaps after a while the idea that there were wider choices about more fundamental decisions would be masked. "Organized free play" within the allotted half hour reflected the market mentality of consumer sovereignty in its early form.

Performance

Among the many functions that the playground was to perform was the responsibility of bringing together vast numbers of children and then separating them again. In a way similar to that observed by Marx when he noted that industrialization had the effect of socializing the means of production and atomizing the working class, the playground gathered children in from all corners of the Lower East Side and then, on the basis of what the clock said, divided them. The clock, in the form of a stopwatch, acted as a judge—condemning those who performed poorly while heralding the superiority of others. The report of the Third National Recreation Congress, held in 1909, states that stopwatches were used in races and previous year's records were "posted up for the children to compete against."[71] The reformers hoped to construct playgrounds based on "an aristocracy of physical excellence"[72] where children would gain a "breadth of view," thus enlarging their horizon to include those outside of her/his class....[73] Applying the same logic to parks, the *New York Times* wrote as early as 1899:

> When young Charles Augustus, whose father is a brick-
> layer, does fancy tricks on roller skates for the edification of
> Miss Flora McFlimsey, aged 11, he is not oppressed by the
> thought of the millions which stand between them or the
> social gulf that divides them. Class distinctions, in fact, are
> not recognized in the park. The only aristocracy there is
> that of prowess.[74]

The effect of organizing the experiences of young children around a focus of activities both regulated and given
value by an elite's sense of time—a time which had shed its
flowing and holistic qualities and had been replaced by
fifteen-minute quarters and tenth-of-a-second hierarchies
—may have been disastrous. How many tens of thousands
of children were readied for the robotized, Taylorized
factory system as a result of accommodating their time
sense to time schedules, play directors, and a stopwatch?
How many children came to accept hierarchy as "natural"
and "just" because they knew the objective impartiality of
the clock's verdict in the form of timed performances? In
the end, with the subordination of man/child to the
machine, in work and/or leisure, time becomes everything
and man nothing. Quantity alone matters as time becomes
quantifiable and filled with quantifiable things. It becomes
space.

The Rationalization of Urban Social Space

When time is transformed into abstract, precisely mea-
sured physical space as it is in Taylor's system, and as it
becomes the norm of society, all social forms are informed
by fragmentation. Humankind is transformed into units of
laborpower and made to labor in its own shadow on behalf
of its own enslavement. The resultant social order is hall-
marked by class and alienation based on the exploitive
nature of the productive process. Social theorist George
Lukacs assayed the impact of this process on both the individual and the community:

> The personality can do more than look on helplessly while
> its own existence is reduced to an isolated particle and fed
> into an alien system. On the other hand, the mechanical
> disintegration of the process of production into its compo-

nents also destroys those bonds that had bound individuals to a community in the days when production was still "organic."[75]

This breaking of communal bonds, this fragmentation of souls and atomization of community can also be viewed in sports terminology as "causing dissension on a team by dividing it against itself." On the Lower East Side this occurred in many shapes and forms. In the world of work, fragmentation (dissension) occurred with the introduction of the "team system" to the clothing industry. By dividing a craft and then cheapening the individual parts, the "team system" was able to lessen the cost of production and "avoid [ing] the demands of labor unions by the employment of [less-skilled] persons."*[76] When it came to land and room to play, the fragmentation and rule of commodities was equally as strong. All of the "Jewish wards" (Seven, Ten, Eleven, Thirteen, and Seventeen on the Lower East Side) were jammed with people. A portion of the Eleventh Ward, for example, "was among the most crowded spots on earth,"[77] with a density per acre of 986.4 in 1894. In 1908 a census revealed that the external crowdings of buildings onto almost every available lot was matched by intense concentration and overcrowding within the buildings themselves. Over 50 percent of 250 typical East Side families slept with three or four to a room.[78] Thus, people were crowded into houses, houses were packed densely onto blocks, and *capn a bissle luft* (catching a little air) in open space or a park was difficult. Indeed, before the construction of Seward and Hamilton Fish parks in 1903, there were only 64.654 acres of parkland below Fourteenth Street, a scant 2.55 percent of the total area.[79]

Dividing the working class against itself by increasing competition for jobs and packing people like pickles into densely crowded blocks and buildings served the needs of capital well. Wedges were driven among the powerless, and the powerless responded with horizontal violence—vio-

---

*The cost of production for a coat dipped from $2.50–$3.00 previously paid the journeyman tailor to a total of $1.50–$2.00 for five people working in concert. Dividing a craft cheapens the individual parts and simultaneously destroys all-around skills, bringing into being new skills and occupations that correspond to the need for profit and control.

lence directed against one another instead of the oppressor. The drunkenness, the wife beating, and the suicides that were a daily occurrence on the Lower East Side, and which continue today in urban ghettos, were the direct result of this fragmentation and compartmentalization. Repulsed and frightened at immigrant street life and its relationship with the Socialist and anarchist movements, the elite fought hard to break the "team spirit" of the workers. This desire for segmentation and control reached its fulfillment and highest stage of development in the design and development of children's playgrounds.

A Fence

"There are certain fundamental necessities which should go with every city [play]ground," wrote the New York City Recreation Bureau in 1910. "These are: First, fence; Second, shelter; Third, toilet; Fourth, water." The playground without a fence was seen as "a source of continued and expensive annoyance and disorder."[80] Two years earlier, an article in *The Playground* asked, "Should a playground always be fenced?" The answer came back somewhat rhetorically: "The greater the congestion, the higher and stronger should be the fences...the two factors, congestion and fence, varying in exact proportion." Fences were needed "so that roughs could be kept out, property not destroyed and boisterousness and obscenity made difficult."[81] Thus, the first function of the fence was to isolate those who had been selected for salvation from those who were still considered cultural heathens. Simultaneously, a second function would be realized—transforming the playground into a total institution during the hours the children were in its confines. The supervisors and their assistants would control time, conduct, language, movement, and modes of social interaction. The fence would assist these efforts as the material side of an authoritarian structure.

If the fence was to help compartmentalize the experience of young working-class children by separating play from life, the playground from the "evil" street, leisure time from other time, and if it was to assist in the "many problems of discipline"[82] confronting the play leader, the fence was to serve still a third function—to stratify and fragment even those who accepted its legitimacy. The fence (or shrubbery) was employed as a barrier demarcating space which was allocated according to age and sex. The PAA Committee on Equipment wrote:

> The kind of apparatus to be placed in a given playground must be determined by the ages and sex of the patrons.... The ideal arrangement then, is one of three separate and distinct play spaces. The next best arrangement is a separate play space for boys above ten years, and a second play space for girls of all ages and children of both sexes under ten years. The poorest arrangement...is a single play space for both sexes and all ages.[83]

These divisions corresponded to the theories of G. S. Hall and Joseph Lee, both of whom believed that children developed by various stages of growth where certain modes of behavior predominate and where the evolutionary history of the human race is "recapitulated." Each age supposedly calls forth the need for different responses to various instincts which have been held over from different periods of race development. As Lee said:

> In the development of the growing child, potential faculties in the form of instinctive impulses appear, each in its turn, asking to be woven into the fabric of his life....[84]

Both Hall and Lee also believed in the innate inferiority of women, although Lee was a bit more liberal in his willingness to grant them parity with boys in sports, at least up to the age of thirteen, at which time puberty, romantic love, and motherhood superseded athletics. Hall was less kind:

> Real virtue requires enemies, and women and effeminate and old men want placid, comfortable peace, while a real man rejoices in noble strife....[85] [For girls:] It is hard for them to bear defeat in games with the same dignity and unruffled temper as boys. They may be a little in danger of being roughened by boyish ways and especially by the crude and unique language.[86]

As a result, playgrounds were designed to provide athletics for older boys and activities for girls, space for older boys—

for baseball, running games, and football, and shade for girls—so as to protect their delicate complexions. The foremost authority on playground equipment in the country, E. B. DeGroot, a man who lectured far and wide on the proper construction and equipping of playgrounds, made one of his strongest recommendations a plea for a shaded, separate section for little children and girls because "Even young girls are thoughtful concerning their complexion and seem unable to endure the direct rays of the sun in the same manner that boys seem able to endure it."[87]

A Picture of Captivity

The fenced playground took as inevitable the divisions between the sexes and ages. It assumed that older boys needed space to realize virtue so they were allotted at least 50 percent of the grounds while the girls and small children made do with the rest. This was logical to the reformers because they believed that athletics were valuable for a woman primarily insofar as they made of her "a companion for her husband on the golf course and a playmate with her children."[88] The district superintendent of schools in New York City, Edward Stitt, claimed that "Separate playgrounds for boys and girls are very advisable," and noted that the Department of Education used separate school entrances to simplify the separation problem. Once inside, the sexes were joined for assembly "as the singing is greatly improved by the girls' voices, and it is also advisable to have the playground as a unit for such patriotic exercises as the 'Salute to the Flag' and the singing of national songs."[89] Everyone then was equally an American but not equally human: girls were voices and complexions on the way to being mothers, boys were what the game was all about.

The equipment on each side of the playground revealed the superiority–inferiority distinctions perceived as "natural" and perpetuated as "inevitable." On the boys' side there was a running track, a 100-yard-dash straightaway, a softball field, basketball courts, jumping pits, and ample space for all games. There was apparatus equipment consisting of vaults, parallel bars, high and low swings, seesaws, and teeter ladders. Activity and competition were the bywords of the space allocated for boys. Conversely, the watchwords for the girls' space were relaxation and cooperation. Girls were provided with softball and basketball courts, but the organized play leaders were not too serious about girls playing softball or basketball. In fact, the sketch provided as a model in *The Playground* also had a wading pool in the middle of the courts. Additional space was there for croquet, ring games, and apparatus work. A canvas-covered awning was to provide shelter for a sand table, benches, baby hammocks, blocks and toys, and other child-care tools. Of course, not every playground in every city's recreation system adhered exactly to these suggestions. There were regional and historical differences according to availability of land and changing attitudes about coeducational play. (The PAA softened its ideology on coed play past puberty at the same time that the Socialist and feminist movements were peaking. In New York City, this softening even went so far as to allow for the development of an evening recreation center that permitted mixed dancing—but only under the strictest of supervision.) But, by and large, playgrounds followed the norms of compartmentalized experiences at a time when the immigrants were ripe for creating wholly new social approaches.

With the development of sophisticated means of production that could allow for the creation of a "leisure-time" problem came the upper-class effort to contain it. The containment was both figurative and literal as fences were built around minds and open lots. Time was transfigured from a natural-religious phenomenon into a form of currency that was "spent" by the masses who could neither retain control of their own temporal schemes nor successfully fend off the imposition of patterns set down by the propertied class. This is not to say that they did not try, but because they lacked control over the means of production that ultimately determined the pace and position of class life, their efforts were reduced to escapism or accepting their employer's categories and fighting back—for shorter hours, work weeks, etc.—within these categories.

At the turn of the century there were great labor fairs attended by tens of thousands of people, mass parades celebrating strikes and workers' holidays, and autonomous street-life culture. The Lower East Side was alive with the sights and sounds of immigrant cultural institutions such as the *landsmanschaftn* and the Workmen's Circle, and with cafes, theaters, street-corner rallies. But the perpetuation of these institutions as centers of autonomous working-class culture depended on intergenerational transmission of values and concerns—for labor, Socialist or anarchist, and Jewish forms. The development of capitalism and the rise of organized play limited such transmissions. Instead of immigrant children growing up with these institutions imbued with working class and immigrant traditions and values, they were being carted off and isolated on playgrounds, in settlement houses, and in vacation schools. Reformers like David Blaustein, headworker at the Educational Alliance, considered immigrant parents ignorant of the values of proper play. "The whole idea of play is foreign to immigrant people—a waste of time, frivolity,"[90] Blaustein was fond of saying. Thus, their children would have to be educated in play despite their parents' protestations, and with this education the umbilical cord to street culture and working-class/immigrant traditions was severed.

The tempo of Taylorism carried through into everyday life, making it a time of speed and ephemerality. Harry Roskolenko saw that

> it was time for speed, not for permanent values. It was the time for mass living, mass production, mass consumption....[91]

The Jewish immigrants of the Lower East Side were ultimately worn down by such massing, and with the limited resources available they concentrated on the most immediate concerns of exploitation—those at the point of production. Meanwhile, through compartmentalization of space and the destruction of immigrant cultural rhythms, capital outflanked them. A picture of the whole, a memory of the past was lost, and as a result so were the immigrants.

To be a true woman means to be yet more mother than wife . . . . The elimination of maternity is one of the greatest calamities, if not diseases, of our age.

—G. Stanley Hall

CHAPTER 6 Sex, Sport, and Suppression

Perhaps the most important aspect of the organized-play movement was the effect it had on the relations between men and women. On the playgrounds, in the play journals, and through "The Normal Course of Play" Lee, Hall, the settlement house workers, and others relegated men and women to different and unequal statuses. Girls and women were treated as "the future mothers of sons,"[1] while boys and young men were socialized to be virile in line with the belief that "the world's dearest possession is manhood."[2] The list of stereotypes used to describe or explain the differences between males and females is staggering:

> Women don't inherit the throwing coordination nor the striking coordination in a developed form....This deficiency puts girls at a physical disadvantage in games from early childhood.[3]

> Girls are content to sit and have the subject matter pumped into them by recitations etc., and to merely accept, while boys are more inspired by being told to do things and make and test experiments.[4]

> Women have lacked skill in fulfilling the wider and less personal relationships.[5]

As a direct result of the play movement's unequal treatment of males and females, women were effectively "locked out of the ballpark." As feminist Emma Goldman noted, they were burdened with overcoming "an inferior past and present physical training...at the expense of their physical and psychical well-being."[6] Conversely, for men sports became a major distraction, diverting their attention from their understanding of class society and the exploitation they suffered within it.

The stereotypes and patterns of inequality that tainted the relationship between men and women in society at large filtered down into the organized-play movement. A vicious cycle was created whereby the attitudes that sustained sexual ignorance and patriarchy in adult society bred attitudes and organized-play programs for youngsters which reinforced the initial distortions. It was as if the playground movement had undertaken the task of being responsible for initiating through play the sexist beliefs and behaviors which would be completed at a later point in a child's life.

In order to understand how and why the organized-play movement acted the way it did toward sexuality, and to understand the ramifications of the movement's impact on youth, it is necessary to analyze sex and work in America in the Progressive Era. Only by doing this can we develop an adequate understanding of the body, and it is only through an understanding of the body that we develop a theory capable of analyzing these issues.

A Material Base

The body serves many functions. It is the vehicle through which we feel sexual arousal and fulfillment. It serves as the basic equipment of sports production. And in capitalist societies, it is the selling of one's body to another for the purpose of making profit (surplus value) that is the foundation of work. In the process of realizing itself in a sexual, playful, or productive way, the body enters into a relationship with others and creates community. Building a community with other humans allows for the satisfaction of these biological needs, and within that community such biological needs as sex, food, and sustenance take on a social character. The kinds and amounts of food that are eaten, the sexual opportunities and taboos that develop, and the character of everyday life is affected by the nature of the community; the nature of the community is determined by the work of its members. There is, in effect, a cycle which moves from the body (and its needs) to the creation of a community (and the satisfaction of those needs) and back to the body (where the satisfaction is determined by the body's work and interaction with others).

In the Jewish communities of Eastern Europe, the patterns of work that linked people to one another included commerce, skilled labor, artisanship and manual labor. Both men and women provided for the economic well-being of their families using both their minds and bodies to generate income. There existed a semblance of unity between intellectual and manual labor, between mind and body. According to Zboroski and Herzog:

> Even a manual worker claims that his muscles are directed by head work....Artisans are constantly pointing out the intellectual demands of their labor. "You must put some head into it," they say...no work is considered "headless" by the one who does it...[7]

Shtetl society was shaped accordingly. There were classes, but class distinctions were not nearly as sharp as those in America. Women were treated as less than the equals of men, but that inequality was tempered by their full participation in the economy and other social realms. Play was different and distinct from work or study, but it was neither compartmentalized nor conscripted by a division of the world into rigid categories of mind and body, work and play. These distinctions grew and hardened in America.

In the United States these Jewish immigrants found Taylorism in vogue. Piece-work, time and motion studies, and talk of efficiency was everywhere—in the home (domestic engineering), on the job (scientific management), and even in play (physical efficiency). But in the midst of all this clamor about efficiency and management, the truth remained that Taylorism was widening the gap between minds and bodies, classes, men and women, labor and leisure. By reducing work to a time and motion equation Taylorism reduced workers to mere bodies and removed thought from their realm. The conceptual functions of labor were transferred from the factory floor to the manager's office. Workers were divorced from any effective control over the means of production as their rate of work, their style of work, and even their knowledge of how things worked became the prerogative of management.

The rupture enforced by Taylor's stopwatch and time sheets created two spheres. The first was one of action, decision, power, and reflection—in a word, control. It was the world of management, of capital. The other was a sphere of subservience, reaction, acquiescence—in a word, impotence. It was the sphere of the worker. The worker was the body who daily sold his sweat, muscle, and blood in order to survive. The capitalist, on the other hand, practiced and planned ever anew to increase his profits. He existed as a mind, developing new techniques of production in order to achieve more effective control, increase efficiency, and improve profits.

The effects of this mind-body split and its hardening into social roles were manifold. They affected all aspects of social life. The dividing line between childhood and maturity was drawn ever more starkly. Work was purged of its playful elements as standardization and synchronization flourished. But most important was the effect the mind-body split had on the relations between the sexes. Working-class men, who were exploited as mindless bodies at work, reacted by playing their familial roles as "minds"— acting, making decisions, and controlling women and children. For men, women became mere bodies, to be abused in many of the same ways that men themselves were abused at work. Women, in fact, became the generalized bodies of society: they became "objects."[8] The object was a body which was both praised (as a reproductive organ) and repressed (as a productive power).

Men and women both tried to reconstitute themselves as complete (mind and body) human beings, but the opportunities to do so were limited for them and ever-shrinking for their sons and daughters who were being taught through organized play to view these roles as "natural." Work was pictured as the sphere of men; women were consigned to the home. In each institution men and women had only the narrowest chances for total fulfillment. Only in the absence of the oppressor could each assume some degree of reconstituted wholeness. When men were at work during the day, women could "rule the roost." When the foreman was away or out of sight, or when there was a strike, men could "take matters into their own minds." And in extreme circumstances such as war or economic booms or while unmarried, women could even enter the paid labor force. But, in the main the capital-labor split enhanced by Taylorism worked to subvert the unity of men and women and distort the social patterns of the working class.

Victorian Morality

Taylorism affected the body through work, and as such it had the greatest impact on the character of everyday life. But the body (and therefore society) was also informed by the nature of sexuality during the late 1800s and early 1900s. That "nature" has been described as "Victorian morality" and was composed of a conspiracy of silence and a double standard. The conspiracy of silence considered sex and sexuality a prohibited topic, and the double standard provided one set of social norms for men and another less equal set for women. Thus, Victorian morality functioned to maintain sex tension, oppression, and ignorance by mystifying and limiting the body. Because of the conspiracy of silence and the double standard brothels flourished, information about birth control was scarce, and sexual anguish was enshrined as a social constant.

At the turn of the century, however, Victorian morality came under attack from two directions, from the "sophisticates and rebellious intellectuals" of the period and by a "purity movement"[9] of doctors and reformers. Indepen-

dently and sometimes antagonistically, these two groups
set out to reformulate Americans' attitudes toward sex and
the body, work and play. The intellectuals (many of whom
came from the Lower East Side) worked to create a climate
of freedom about the body and sexuality, while the doctors
and reformers concentrated on countering the rising divorce rate and saving the family. Each group understood
that sexual innocence was sexual ignorance. Ignorance was
a threat, either to a classless society or the perpetuation of
class society—depending upon how you looked at it. Emma
Goldman, who typified the "rebels'" thinking on this topic,
put the matter succinctly when she argued for the consign-
ment of Victorian morality to the dustbin of history. She
wrote:

> the relation of the sexes must be freed from the oppressing
> fetters of a lame morality that degrades every human emo-
> tion to the plane of utility and purpose.

Regarding the physical limitations which were a woman's
norm, she said:

> Everything within her that craves assertion and activity
> should reach its fullest expression; and all artificial barriers
> should be broken and the road towards freedom cleared of
> every trace of centuries of submission and slavery.[10]

Rebels like Emma Goldman, Margaret Sanger, Bernarr Mac-
Fadden, and Dr. Benzion Liber thought that girls and
women should be free to love, to run, to jump, to play un-
inhibitedly and to explore. Conversely, Prince A. Morrow,
founder of the Society of Sanitary and Moral Prophylaxis,
worried not about new freedom for women but about preserving patriarchy. His reform organization appealed to the
public's "concern about preserving the family" and about
"the divorce problem." His organization and others like it
campaigned *against* prostitution and suggestive literature,
for male continence, and was frightened by "the spread of
diseases which have their origin in the Social Evil."[11] The
reformers were less concerned about freedom for women
than they were about "free love."

The Conspiracy of Silence

Both the radicals and the reformers attacked the conspiracy of silence with a vengeance—fighting to eradicate incorrect folk beliefs concerning venereal disease and conception. But whereas the reformers rallied around the banner of continence and declared that it was "entirely compatible with health,"[12] the radicals asserted that a freer sexuality would result in a healthier (and therefore more revolutionary) worker. The question of sexuality was closely intertwined with the Woman's Question and while the reformers supported suffrage, the radicals went much further. Margaret Grant, for example, deplored "modesty" as a "code word for silence. Some of the rules of modesty," she noted, "lead to ill-health and physical weakness, so that few women are well because of them." She argued that women "will never have good health until we throw modesty to the winds, and conduct ourselves like some of those shameless creatures who really seem to glory in their sex."[13]

Grant, Goldman, Sanger, Liber, and MacFadden were supported by thousands of followers and by "authors of fiction and drama [who] with increasing frequency were suggesting that a woman has a sexual existence."[14] Consequently, for the first two decades of the new century, fierce battles were fought over definitions of "obscene." The propertied class considered the discussion of birth control, the allusion that women were sexual beings, and the portrayal of nudity in art as obscene, immoral, and indecent. The reformers—drawn mainly from that class—worried about the obscenity of prostitution, pornography, and the dissemination of information about sex from "foul sources," which included quack doctors, degenerates, and "misinformed playmates."[15] The radicals' definition of obscenity and immorality cut to the core of an "immoral society." The cruel exploitation of men, women, and children at the hands of the "merciless Moloch of capitalism;"[16] the denial of female equality, sexuality, and freedom; and the prudishness of a repressive class society—these were the obscene and immoral pillars which bolstered the conspiracy of silence and the double standard.

The Double Standard

The double standard was everywhere. In the sweatshops, at home, and on the playground females were expected to conform to one set of values and males to another. As the very first issue of Margaret Sanger's *Woman Rebel* put it, women were enslaved by "the machine, by wage slavery, by bourgeois morality, by customs, laws and superstitions."[17] Radicals like her and Emma Goldman opposed this double standard which coincidentally was being given new intellectual life through the "penis envy" theory of Freud— a theory which gained an audience in the U.S. thanks to playground ideologist G. Stanley Hall, who as president of Clark University arranged for Freud to come to America and elaborate his ideas.

Both Sanger and Goldman recognized that the double standard and the conspiracy of silence led to the commoditization of women as mothers and prostitutes, and that it contributed to their physical inferiority and weaknesses. Goldman claimed that the reformers who railed against prostitution were not concerned that "a woman sells her body [marriage] but, rather that she sells it to many." The problem of the trade in women as she saw it was "exploitation," and the enemy was "capitalism that fattens on unpaid labor, thus driving thousands of women and girls into prostitution." If women were given more information about their bodies and if as girls they were allowed more freedom to play and explore, argued the radicals, prostitution could be attacked more effectively—in its legal and illegal forms.

The radicals linked the sexual double standard to the double standard of exploitation and capitalism. Everywhere, and by every measure, they argued, women came out on the short end of the stick. The story was the same whether in the garment industry or in the organized play movement. In the shops women "suffered from petty persecutions and the failure of employers and managers to recognize the girls as human beings.'" In the organized play movement they were limited in their activities as girls and discriminated against as employees. They were given titles (playground attendants) different from those given men (gym attendants) and even though the work was the same, they received a lower pay. The double standard and the conspiracy of silence combined—at work and play—to create a Victorian moral order that made the pursuit of equality, independence, or even physical effectiveness for women, a near impossibility.

Fashion and Physical Disability

Taylorism, the conspiracy of silence, and the double standard contributed to molding the immigrants' consciousness about the body and therefore about work, about sexuality, and ultimately about play. Some of these influences were new and shocking to the East European Jews, but some were not. Many of the patterns of sex separation which existed in America had been a part of *shtetl* life. The *cheder* (school) of Eastern Europe was a sex-segregated institution and there were numerous other avenues of life where sexism flourished. But immigration meant a major change in lifestyle and world view for hundreds of thousands of Jews, and this could have carried over to the area of sex roles. A new and more egalitarian pattern of sexual identities could have evolved in the New World just as new patterns of work and play had developed. Restrictiveness could have been transcended. Instead, Americanization meant legitimization of those patterns of sexual exclusion, and the authority and aura of the new country sanctioned a segment of *shtetl* culture as an abstraction. Relations between the sexes could have been better, fairer; instead they were different, but only in the sense that they were unconnected to the more sex-egalitarian context within which they had existed. The Old World traits of sexual separation and female inferiority were transplanted to a structurally different soil, fertilized by a developing monopoly capitalism, and tended by schoolteachers, play directors, cops, and fashion designers.

Fashion, in the Progressive Era, played a major role in physiologically handicapping women. It was laden with the message of women's innate infirmity. Its purpose was to package a woman as an object too frail to control her own destiny and requiring the assistance of men for that purpose. As social critic Thorsten Veblen noted in his *Theory of the Leisure Class,*

> the high heel, the skirt, the impracticable bonnet, the corset, and the general disregard of the wearer's comfort, which is an obvious feature of all civilized women's apparel, are so many items of evidence to the effect that in modern civilized scheme of life the woman is still, in theory, the economic dependent of the man—that, perhaps in a highly idealized sense, she is still the man's chattel. . . . [18]

No one item of clothing more effectively demonstrated the chattel-like nature of women's status than the corset.

The corset was a close-fitting woman's undergarment, tightened with lace and reinforced with stays. A woman in a corset had her waist severely constricted, her breathing impaired, and thus presented the physical image of beauty and helplessness that fit the ideology of woman's inferiority as snugly as the garment fit madam. By 1914, the U.S. corset industry had 126 establishments, 20,496 wage earners, $23.8 million in capital, and $40.5 million in value of products.[19] Its product was a well-accepted fact of life for millions of American women and women wanting to "Americanize."

Physical culturist Bernarr MacFadden claimed that the corset destroyed womanhood, motherhood, beauty, health, and sex instincts. He averred that the corset pinched the waist, destroyed the uterus, restricted lung development, and weakened or sometimes killed unborn babies. "Beware of opium fiends, alcohol tipplers and corset-crushed wrecks!" he warned.[20] For the first years of his magazine *Physical Culture,* he listed the corset curse as the number one impediment to the proper physical development of the American people.

If the corset curse was not quite as serious as MacFadden felt it to be, it was still a major element in the perpetuation of sexist stereotypes and the physical restrictions placed on women. Along with other restrictive women's fashions of the period, the corset symbolized to men, and concretely demonstrated to women, that motion, physical power, and competence were not of her realm.*ᵃAs Veblen put it, the purpose of the corset and "other mutilations and contrivances" was to decrease "the visible efficiency of the individual" by arguing physical disability in the wearer.[21]

Domestic Science

If men and women were expected to have radically different adult roles then it followed that each sex must undergo extremely different socialization experiences. Nowhere was this truer than in the organized-play activities designed for boys and girls at the turn of the century. There were different games for and different approaches taken toward males and females. With the rise of organized play came institutions like the Camp Fire Girls, Boy Scouts, the PAA, and settlement-run "homes" that played important roles in stereotyping men and women. In line with the developing needs of capital, these organizations developed structures and ideologies through which the socialization of children became the progressive socialization of alienation. In the second issue of *Mother Earth*, Emma Goldman raised this issue in an article entitled "The Child and Its Enemies":

> Is the child to be considered as an individuality, or as an object to be molded according to the whims and fancies of those about it?
> The child shows its individual tendencies in its plays, in its questions, in its associations with people and things. [But] It must become a thing, an object. Its questions are

---

*Although the bicycle craze of the late nineteenth century (which was in good measure a women's phenomenon) loosened some of the Victorian dress restrictions that served as norms for middle-, upper-, and lower-class women, it was still necessary for the *New York Times* to editorialize in 1895 that women were bipeds too (just like men) and that the bloomer costume should be accepted as it allowed for a woman to use both her legs. In 1897, Eleanor Penrose was arrested and passed the night in jail for wearing slacks on Coney Island. She received a parting injunction from the court to change her attire. In Chicago, squads of police traveled along the beachfronts as late as 1910, measuring the distance from the neck to a woman's swimsuit neckline, arresting for indecent exposure all those whose garbs were considered obscene.

met with narrow, conventional, ridiculous replies mostly
based on falsehoods....

...every effort in our educational life seems to be
directed toward making of the child a being foreign to
itself...[shaped] to best fit into the treadmill of society and
the emptiness and dullness of our lives.[22]

In order to mold young girls to the dullness of the home,
domestic science programs were developed. Such programs
were intended to advance a girl's domesticity, enhance her
femininity, and "cultivate a taste for those domestic virtues
that tend to make home-life happier and brighter."[23]
Domestic science and cooking classes were supposed to
introduce working-class girls and adolescent women to the
"joys of cooking"—and sewing, washing, and mothering. No
settlement house was without a premotherhood program;
no playground denied any young girl the opportunity to
develop her "natural differentiations."[24] Each program was
designed to ameliorate the collapse of family life which in
turn threatened the domestic order and class society. For
every girl like Lilian Skupsky who "spent every Friday afternoon with my mother" learning to "cook and bake,"[25] the
wealthy feared that there were scores of other children who
were not learning such skills and who would ostensibly fail
as mothers in later years. Young girls who became mothers
and were deficient cooks and homemakers, so the thinking
went, would raise children with "poor eating habits." These
children would go in one of two directions: either they
would satisfy their hunger with habit-forming foods (like
pickles) that would lead, ultimately, to alcoholism; or they
would remain malnourished and become sick, an inefficient worker, a public charge. Both developments were a
threat to society's stability and so the elite seeking to shore
up their hold on this massing urban world, developed
school lunch programs (as an immediate palliative) and
domestic science classes or premotherhood programs (as a
long-range strategy).[26]

Through these various domestic programs, young girls
were taught the rudiments of homemaking, sewing,
cooking, gardening, etc.,[27] but their instruction came
wrapped in an ideological package aimed at teaching them

to "brush away the dull gray coating of the apparent daily drudgery and revive the inherent romance, achievement and adventure of human life."[28] True, some feminists "began to apply scientific management to the home" which would become "freed from mere tradition and social custom" under the "principles of domestic engineering."[29] But considered in full, the effect was more repressive than liberating. Women in model flats,[30] on the playgrounds, in the Camp Fire Girls, and in domestic science classes were to become parts of a "universal community of mother-hood,"[31] as Gulick put it. By learning what G. Stanley Hall called "the rudiments of household chemistry,"[32] domesti-city, child study, pedagogy and maternity, she could play her divinely ordained role of properly forming the child from "an undeveloped germ."[33]

Building Busts

In order to mold her child correctly from an undeveloped germ, a female first had to shape herself. An article in the *New York Times* of April 1899 revealed the extent to which this process of self-formation was accepted as a significant part of a woman's maturation. A story is told of a group of young women who are discussing swimming—not the demands of the sport or the challenge of humans testing themselves against nature, or the like. What was discussed was one girl's considered opinion that swimming "is the best kind of exercise to develop the chest. I know a girl," she continued, "whose chest simply expanded inches after she began to swim and she grew as pretty as a picture." Swimming was credited not only with having silicon-like powers but also with helping this girl walk differently and become the type of girl that "people like so much." The sport "made her life worth living for her." Coyly, either the journalist or the young woman who is credited with the conversation remarks: "Oh, by the way, I had forgotten, she's going to be married next week. And all on account of her swimming too. She was one of the few girls who look pretty in the water and after they come out of it." Mr. Right, who has "lots of money and [is] handsome," took one look at our protagonist and—yes, it's true, "fell head over heels in love with her."[34] Thus, even when sport was admitted as a part of a young girl's world, it was connected to femininity, domesticity, and the pursuit of wifehood.

Of course, not every woman could be so lucky, but at least she could try. All she needed to do was follow a simple formula: swim, develop a larger chest and proper walk, become popular, find the spouse of her dreams, marry. This was the advice of organized-play leaders like G. Stanley Hall who was an avid enthusiast of swimming and other chest-building exercises like rope climbing. Hall, Luther Gulick, and the others saw a role for such activities as antibodies in their fight against radicals who disparaged maternity and marriage. Although most of the leaders of the movement did not take their commitment to marriage and motherhood quite as "scientifically" as Gulick, who as an adolescent prepared a list of requirements for a wife, they nevertheless did see the matter as quite serious.[35] After all, they believed that "the world's dearest possession is manhood" and that women as wives and mothers had the responsibility of reproducing, physically and psychically, the next generation of males.[36] This was hardly a simple chore, because men were competitive savages who required taming and training by the fairer sex. Hall wrote:

> Evolutionists tell us that woman has domesticated and educated savage man and taught him all his virtues by exercising her royal prerogative of selecting in her mate just those qualities that pleased her....If so, she is still engaged in this work as much as ever.[37]

How was a woman to exercise her "royal prerogative" and which virtues was she to teach her "savage man"? First, as a wife she was to exhibit "the power to please, to amuse, to soothe and sympathize"[38]—all skills she was to learn through her girls' clubs and domestic science classes at the settlement or on the playground. Second, as a mother she was to "organize simple constructive games and direct [the] intelligent play [of her children]." This she could do if the playground had performed its task correctly by keeping "the play instinct alive in girls for the sake of the little children who may come to them later.[39] Finally, women as wives and mothers were to act on Hall's conception of play as "a school of ethics." They would be ethical instructors, teaching their sons the ideals of fair play, competition as a manly art, hierarchy, and obedience. In every instance of their work they were aided by an American ideology which labeled males as rough and aggressive and an organized-play movement that raised such characteristics to virtues.

Ferocity and Football

In his poignant autobiography, Marcus Ravage who grew up on the Lower East Side provides a stark example of the physical attitudes so highly valued by a culture which puts a premium on distancing. He tells of his summer vacation back in the ghetto after spending the fall, spring, and winter months away at college. Upon his return, he is greeted by his brother at the ferry. The brother rushes toward Marcus and, with joy in his heart, hugs and kisses him. Ravage asks rhetorically, "Did I kiss him back?" Within his answer is our key: "I am afraid not." Months at the University of Missouri had taught him only too well that "The genuine American recognized but one distinction in human society —the vital distinction between the strong, effective, 'real' man and the soft, pleasure-loving unreliant failure."[40] This anecdote shows that socialization toward manhood required that men regard other males with affection only at great risk; physical intimacy, even within the family, could lead to a psychological inability to remain aloof and economically calculating. Therefore, intramale intimacy had to be replaced with the manly American traits of emotional reserve and physical competitiveness.

Football was praised as a sport precisely because it was said to develop these "manly traits": "Football is for the strong, it encourages the 'fighting instinct.' Show me a successful man and in nine cases out of ten he will be what is termed a 'fighter.' If you wish your boys to be men—real men...encourage them to play football."[41] In football, the emphasis on bodily contact is transformed from one of tenderness (as in sexuality) to one of rigidity and tightness. Its purpose is to inflict pain and so it is quite well suited to be the inversion of the physical requirements necessary for a loving or sexual relationship. Its structure, the violence, the animosity, the unbridled aggression make it a physical paradigm of asceticism. The Socialist newspaper the *Jewish Daily Forward*, which supported the idea of immigrants learning baseball to become better Americans, denounced football. Abe Cahan, the *Forward's* influential editor, was repulsed by football's violent nature and its elitism—it was mainly played in private colleges. Cahan called football "a wild, aristocratic game,"[42] and dismissed it out of hand. But the upper class loved it. If everyone wouldn't play football, then at least everyone should be football fans, or so they thought. Football would put an end to those mannerisms that made for "softness."

Softness was also to be combatted in those character laboratories known as playgrounds. There, play leaders were constantly reminded that "no institution is more important than that which turns out manly men.[43] And in times of peace as well as in times of war, a manly man was a warlike man, bred of a bellicose boy. Thus, the entire issue of *The Playground* in July of 1912 was devoted to the theme "Martial Virtues Conserved Through Play." Not surprisingly, play was defined as the "child of war"; boys were seen as having an "innate pugnacity"; and the need of play directors was laid out quite clearly:

> We must make new energies and hardihood, continue the manliness to which the military mind so faithfully clings. Martial virtues must be enduring cement. Intrepidity, contempt of softness, surrender of private interests, obedience to command, must remain the rock upon which states are built, unless, indeed we wish for dangerous reactions against the commonwealth fit only for contempt and liable to invite attack....[44]

In short, men must be desensitized psychologically as well as physically, and separated from women. Only by doing this would the state and private property be secure from the threat posed by a social philosophy of equality—sexual, political, and economic. Lee himself wrote that "Play involves pain....Subordination, not selfishness, is the characteristic of true play."[45] He also saw fighting as one of the seven play instincts (along with creation, rhythm, hunting, nurture, curiosity, and team play). The logical conclusion to all this worship of martial virtues on an institutional level was the involvement of the PAA during World War I as a part of a War Camp Community Service, providing recreation and moral support to state-side soldiers.[46]

On an individual basis, the results were quite more dramatic. Men became psychologically crippled, handicapped in their ability to reach out to women and one another with affect and in a spirit of equality. Although they seemed to be freer in their bodily movements, their range of motion was indeed constricted by the same stereotypes that limited women. Men were the other side of the coin. If women were to be dainty, graceful "birds," men had to be powerful, plodding "animals." The cult of manliness created a vicious cycle for men wherein they were forced to see themselves as aggressive, domineering, and "in control." Since working-class men were pathetically not the shapers of most of their own destinies, they sought narrower spheres in which they could be potent. The home, the bar, and the brothel became castles within which every man could be a king, ruling queens.*

Sex Tension

In order for men to become "real men," desirous of ruling women and thereby solidifying the stability of the family and hence the state, the theorists of the organized-play movement believed it necessary to develop and maintain a psychological trait they called "sex tension." Sex tension was considered "one of the subtlest and most potent of all psychological agencies"[47] which involved sublimation on the one hand and seduction on the other. Sublimation was required, so the theorists believed, because an overindulgence of sex would lead to an unleashing of wild and unmanageable emotions. Joseph Lee wrote:

> There cannot be too much love in the world, but there is such a thing as Too Much Love-Making; it is not properly a

---

*Although men do not directly rule women in bars, their antifemale language and banter is a symbolic equivalent of physical domination.

routine occupation, and if too steadily pursued it will generate more emotions than can safely be handled.[48]

Seductiveness was required, according to Lee, Hall, and the others, because the family had to be reproduced in every generation in order to insure the viability of the system.

In order to insure the continued existence of "sex tension," the PAA developed programs for the playgrounds, schools, and recreation centers that would "make boys more manly and girls more womanly."[49] For girls, this involved developing poise and control over their bodies[50] and being taught "the dignity and beauty of good form in play."[51] This translated into an activities program that in athletics called for softball, dodge ball, relay races, medicine ball, and prisoner's base—all games that did not provide an image of commotion or too many girls active at once. Field hockey and even basketball were considered too strenuous for young girls.[52] Track and field was prohibited; interscholastic games were likewise banned; and the general public was barred from those girls' games that were held. A few years after the athletic badge tests had been developed for boys, tests for girls were developed and then revised; they involved only such activities with dignity and grace as potato races, balancing, and shooting basketball goals. So completely was the ideology of femininity and womanhood accepted as an undifferentiated whole, as every woman forever the same,[53] that the girls' badge tests did not even have categories of age, weight, or height.

The most significant aspect of the move to develop and maintain sex tension was the organized-play movement's efforts to curtail coed play. Every play leader, whether a theoretician like Lee or Hall or an administrator like Hetherington or Helen M. McKinstry, believed in eliminating coed play with the onset of puberty. Before a child reached physical maturation, they argued, coed play had benefits that outweighed the dangers, but with puberty should come "a parting of the ways.[54] This apprehension about coed play in puberty could be summed up by the adage "Familiarity breeds contempt." Hall wrote:

> In place of the mystic attractions of the other sex that has inspired so much that is best in the world, familiar comrade-

ship brings a little disenchantment. The impulse to be at one's best in the presence of the other sex grows lax and sex tension remits.... This disillusioning weakens the motivation to marriage....[55]

Since "prolonged familiarity wears down any idealizing influence to the dull monotony of the daily routine"[56] on the one hand, and might encourage lascivious behavior on the other, a play director's vigilance was crucial. The "Normal Course" advised that playground directors should "realize the gravity of the sex problem" and consider the "effects of crowded housing, with the absence of privacy; the temptations of accessible barns and stables and vacant buildings; the dangers of lumber yards and other places of concealment." The play bosses' job was to shape the playground so as to furnish "an opportunity where young people can meet under decent conditions." This was to be accomplished by banning from the grounds all those who were "loose in talk or action," by "constant vigilance" at those times when the sexes did come together, and by reporting to the authorities those things that the director learned through his/her friendship with the children.[57]

The PAA was not alone in its desire to stimulate sex tension by developing activities that would keep the sexes apart and maximize what they considered to be masculine/virile or feminine traits. As early as 1898, the *New York Times Magazine* section was reporting about "summer sunshine parties" organized by churches, kindergartens, mission schools, and public schools for the purpose of teaching about grass, nature, and how to play. The boys had their "baseball, handball, football, 'peel away,'" etc.; the girls had "ropes, hooples, dolls, ring-around-the-rosie and 'mother games.'"[58] In 1904, the Parks Department opened a playground in Tompkins Square Park" exclusively for the use of girls."[59] The Department of Education reserved a third of its evening recreation centers for girls only, while *The Jewish Child*, appealing to a preteen audience, remarked about the beautiful spring weather, "Doesn't it make you want to play ball, if you're a boy, or jump rope and play jacks if you're a girl?" When the same article went on to mention (as a secret) that a certain Ruth sometimes played ball with boys "where she is sure nobody sees her," it remarked that such activities were carried on because when spring is in the air, "she can't help feeling like a little girl again... "[60]

As a little girl Ruth (and her sisters) could afford a certain amount of intense play, but as a young woman, Hall said, there was a danger that she would "take out of her system more than it will bear."[61] Accordingly, females were tracked into activities as much as athletics. The games they played were "less rough" and less vigorous than those of the boys. They were to create visions of form and grace, not visions of power and strength moving through space. The "natural biological inferiority" was taken as a given instead of challenged or scientifically examined. Combined with the restrictions placed on physical contact among men and the demands of fashion (especially corsets), the separation of the sexes and women's subjugation in that process were mightily enhanced by the structure and ideology of PAA play norms. Three generations of Americans are still feeling the impact.

Starting with the body as the material base of sex, sport, and work, we have explored the different histories experienced by men and women of the Progressive Era. The rise of Taylorism created a split between capital and labor that in turn generated a split between men and women. Coupled with the domestic science courses, fashion, play programs, and sexist ideology of the period, these splits worked to create and sustain an image of females as weak and helpless or as sassy and sexy. Men, on the other hand, came to be seen as savages in need of taming, as aggressive, domineering, and in control. Corresponding to these images, the organized-play movement developed an approach to play that involved the separation of males and females, the subjugation of females, and the alienation of all.

Through the separation of the sexes and the subjugation of women, sex tension was maintained. As a result, generations of Americans related to the opposite sex through the prisms of folklore and superstition, advertising, an emerging "romance" literature, and other institutions of a developing consumer culture. The results were a series of encounters and relationships guided as much by distortion and misinformation as by honesty and understanding.

On a societal level American productivity increased, thus making possible the development of an organized-play movement which filled in new, large blocks of leisure time. The increased productivity also made possible, however, the development of working-class culture and the expansion of sexuality. Both the culture and the sexuality were a threat to the social and moral order, so the first was colonized and the second was circumscribed. The body became an instrument of control (rather than one of liberation) as it was divided against the mind and itself; the result was "Work or Play."

To be sure, the industrial capitalist also takes his pleasures. He does not by any means return to the unnatural simplicity of need; but his pleasure is only a side-issue—recreation—something subordinated to production; at the same time it is a calculated and, therefore, itself an economical pleasure. For he debits it to his capital's expense account, and what is squandered on his pleasure must therefore amount to no more than will be replaced with profit through the reproduction of capital. Pleasure is therefore subsumed under capital, and the pleasure-taking individual under the capital-accumulating individual, whilst formerly the contrary was the case.

—Karl Marx
The Economic and Philosophic Manuscripts of 1844

CHAPTER 7 **Selfhood and Property**

Selfhood as possession was the core of the entire ideology of the organized-play movement. Their theorists believed that "the desire to own is one of the strongest passions in the child's life; that selfishness is the rule; that children steal, cheat or lie without scruple to acquire property;" and that these generalizations "will hold almost without exceptions for children under five years, for many children under ten, and in some cases even up to fifteen years of age."[1] These ideas set the stage for viewing alienation as natural, conflict as inevitable, and supervision/control/ coercion as mandatory. Believing that the "child recapitulates the history of the race," the theorists argued that

> Selfishness is the cornerstone of the struggle for existence, deception is at its very foundation, while the acquiring of property has been the most dominant factor in the history of men and nations.[2]

The play ideologues took the existence of private property as a given, never once considering it in a Marxian sense as "the product, the result, the necessary consequence of alienated labor."[3] They failed to distinguish between property which is social by nature (means of production such as factories) and that form of property whose use makes it personal (articles of consumption such as food and clothing). Because they failed to make this distinction, the play theorists were able to enshrine social phenomena like competition, aggression, and class as habits or instincts born of a need to eat, produce, and dress. Competition, aggression, and class were considered part and parcel of biology, facets of instinct. Part of the responsibility of those concerned with play was to give vent to and then mold these instincts in ways which would allow for the child's growth and the society's stability. Children should be taught, for example, "the right," but if this fails, they argued, the child should not be punished. The child should be allowed to be "selfish, lie and cheat, until these natural forces spend themselves." Rank and selfish deeds help to give the child an idea of self, said Lee and Hall; and the child must learn by being selfish and greedy "before he can appreciate ownership in others."[4] With these ideas, a vicious cycle is created whereby history is reduced to mechanistic biology and thereby rendered inaccessible to conscious change.

The play theorists accepted private property as a biological imperative that had been shaped through the various stages of evolution. They believed that the child developed in sequences and that he or she passed through definable stages of biological and psychic growth which paralleled the historical development of humankind: "According to Hall, each stage of individual development was characterized by instincts that were inherited from a corresponding stage of racial bio-cultural organization."[5] With private property as a biological imperative, it followed that strength was equated with accumulation, weakness with cooperation. The play theorists acknowledged that "property was a social before it was an individual sentiment," but they asserted that "the very weakness of man made cooperation a combining of strength and effort, necessary."[6] With these beliefs informing their actions, the leaders of organized play rushed forward to teach hundreds of thousands of children in New York and millions more across the country that weakness is a crime, that cooperation was a form of weakness, and that competition was the key to salvation. But in this new era of trusts and industrial capital, raw, unrestrained competition was inappropriate. To compensate for instances where such competition might breed overintense forms of rivalry on the playground or at work, a twofold strategy emerged.

Again we return to the importance of "instincts" and social order. In the first stage of the strategy the leaders of organized play strove for the development of the "legislative faculty" and of the "judicial faculty" by "having the boys umpire their own games," thus developing what Lee called "social order from within." The boys would agree on boundaries and bases (legislative faculty) and then on calls of safe or out (judicial faculty). This strategy would allow the boys to act as a check on themselves, thus curbing overintense rivalry, and it would also allow them to "feel the pinch of anarchy and the pressing need of overcoming it."[7] In the second stage of the strategy, "team games would be properly supervised by social workers trained in what Hall was fond of calling 'the science of childhood.'"[8] These play leaders would be impartial and honest overseers of the battle for victory. The umpire would "call 'em as he saw 'em" and his word would be law. This institutionalization of umpires meant that although there might be disagreement over the specific instance of a ruling—safe or out, fair or foul—consensus over the basic paradigm of interaction would be secured. The process became a production with set beginnings, trophies, and teams. Playing by the rules became a principle of truth and civilization. But unfortunately for the children, unless they focused on the rules themselves rather than on the umpire's calls, the struggle against the narrowness of organized play would be reduced to an occasional dispute with the inherent contradiction of street play versus organized play subsumed under the cry "Play ball!"

Focusing on the rules themselves was an extremely difficult task. The lure of free equipment, trips to unusual places, and occasional prizes worked to create a desire on the part of many immigrant children to perform acceptably and by the rules. Among workers, upward mobility and the open-shop drives of the employers kept the focus on survival and security, thus taking the heat off capitalism as a structure. There were many children who ignored the playground and continued to brave the hazards of being arrested for street play, just as there were kids who took what they could get from the playground and successfully avoided being seized with its world view. The Socialist and anarchist movements did, of course, encourage a consideration and rejection of the rules, but eventually, as historian James Weinstein points out, social reforms and a more sophisticated approach to conservative trade union leadership operated to circumscribe their influence.[9] Whether at work or at play, an image of the whole (rules, structure, and process) was lost. No one was presumed capable of seeing or accomplishing everything—this was to be the era of the team.

Teamwork

When Playground Association of America president Joseph Lee, psychologist G. Stanley Hall, and other leaders of the organized-play movement talked about "teamwork," they were talking about something quite different from the idea of mutual cooperation in a shared task. Theirs was a teamwork of the assembly line, not the picket line. Lee, for example, wrote glowingly and often about companies that provided recreation and other social welfare benefits to their employees. He congratulated them for "the development of a sense of unity of the worker with the factory" and for having "tried to make the individual employee feel that the work of the company is his work, that what it achieves is his achievement, that he 'belongs' as it were, is a sharer in the larger personality, the unit by which the article is in fact produced."[10]

The larger personality that Lee spoke of could be the factory, America, or, for children, the playground. Everyone was assumed to have a "team instinct" or "belonging instinct" that emerged in the personality around the age of adolescence. It was up to the teachers and play supervisors to provide a stage wherein this instinct could be shaped toward the athletic team, which with its division of labor and varied roles would help train the youngster in the ways of the factory for which he was headed. Describing this socialization, albeit awkwardly, Lee wrote:

> Specialization contributes to the fullness of membership because through it the team makes its full claim on the individual....If the shortstop does not field the ball when it comes his way, if first base does not catch it when it is thrown to him, it will not get fielded or will not be caught. In his own special office each player *is* the team; all there is at that point.[11]

If the success of the entire team was now going to rest on the abilities of each and every participant, be he shortstop or assembly line worker, then the individual needed a thorough schooling in the attributes of teamwork. He (and sometimes she) needed to have a team sense cultivated in the direction of games and not gangs. He needed to strike a balance in his personality between self and society:

> What has brought our race along the road of spiritual development has been the even balance in its composition of the centripetal and centrifugal forces, rendering it certain that neither the socialist nor the individualist shall ever win....[12]

The team experience which flourished during this age of belonging or loyalty simultaneously demanded and taught self-control—"perhaps the most valuable lesson" of the playground—sacrifice, and subordination, "the mark of all morality." Out of this giving of one's self to the cause of the team, comes, according to Lee, "true growth."[13]

The growth Lee had in mind was toward American purity and citizenship, and away from immigrant traditions and culture. He had an antipathy and fear of the European masses that derived from his upbringing as a scion of one of Boston's most prominent and wealthy families. This led him to endorse birth control among and sterilization for the immigrants; as well, he supported immigration restriction.[14] Once the immigrants were here, Lee felt that they should be Americanized as quickly as possible through the combined influence of the school and the organized-play movement. His idea of Americanization, however, meant a denial of class. He wanted social harmony regardless of economics. In fact, he once listed as one of his goals "To make people by education, capable of living...on any amount of money, large or small." If only people would adjust to their situations, he thought, America would be a better place, but he noted with derision, "Very few Americans are capable of doing this."[15] The idea that such an adjustment might be harder for a poverty-stricken immigrant than a millionaire like himself evidently did not occur to him.

Becoming a member of a team and consequently growing toward citizenship was one aspect of the subordination/morality that the PAA president felt was essential to the proper development of a child. Socialization for one's role in the family, which Lee called quite accurately "the first form of the state,"[16] was also an important task of play and a facet of teamwork. But the most important feature of teamwork and the most significant contribution the organized-play movement could make was again regarding work, "the highest form of play."[17] Lee and Hall both saw that modern work did not "satisfy the human instincts as did that industrial system which Mother Nature designed us to pursue."[18] But they believed that the team instinct, of which work was a function, could compensate for the monotony of the job and make it possible for the worker to discharge his responsibility and obligation, his sense of duty:

> When the worker can feel that the factory is his team and its trade-mark is his flag, that he shares the personality embodied in its product, there will come new life both to him and to the industry, incidentally a degree of material success of which we have not yet dreamed.[19]

This team instinct, added Lee, "gives work its special quality" and is the foundation "on which our whole social morality is built."[20]

But if the team instinct was the foundation for work, it was a shaky one. The leaders of the organized-play movement were ambivalent about the progress that came with the modern era. On the one hand Joseph Lee, G. Stanley Hall, Luther Gulick, and the others celebrated the power and achievements of industrialization, the machine. Financially as well as spiritually they shared in the wealth made possible by the expansion of monopoly and the might of America. Yet they feared that the characteristic charm of country life was being sacrificed to urbanization, that the rudimentary satisfaction of work was endangered by overspecialization, and particularly that the child was being subjected to an artificial environment that negated virility, action, and the body at the expense of the mind. Hall wrote that city life was "unnatural" and, "On the whole, the material of the city is no doubt inferior in pedagogic value to country experience."[21] Lee felt that specialization in its modern form was "carried often to so extreme a point... that nothing of significance is left."[22] Work was described as "menial, cheerless, grinding, [and] regular";[23] modern industry, according to Hall, had "largely ceased to be a means of physical development." But modern industry was necessary, even if an evil; industry was the backbone of the economy and the leaders of the organized-play movement accepted that fact. In some ways they sought to accommodate play to the realities of industry; in others they strove to "offset [industry] by compensating modes of activity."[24]

Accommodation

Even as they railed against the stultifying atmosphere of the factory, the leaders of organized play were developing attitudes and activities more suited to the demands of industry than to changing it. Play was considered the best form of manual training because it coordinates bodily functions, produces health, and thereby could produce workers who were strong enough "to endure the indoor confinement"[25] first of schools, then of factories.

"The Normal Course of Play," which was the Playground Association of America's bible, advised that the body should itself be developed "as a machine,"[26] and the association suggested that playgrounds be established so as to improve "the corporate conscience, which is rendered necessary by the complex interdependence of modern life."[27] On most playgrounds there were activities specifically designed to socialize children toward their roles as full-time, full-grown wage earners. There was rafia work, woodworking, and sloyd, a Swedish-designed system of toolwork and manual training. Even those activities that were not specifically preparations for factory work were ruled by the major regulator of factory life, the clock. In accommodating the organized-play movement to industry, the idea was to use play and sport as a way of socializing people to efficiency, sacrifice, and self-control.

Given such an ideology, it was quite natural that amusement would become both a preparation and an after-image for the work process itself, that instead of being a negation or even an escape, leisure would become a prolongation of work. This prolongation was also an introduction for those who like many children had not experienced the factory and therefore had to be molded to accept its definitions of time, space, and relationships. Although F. Winslow Taylor's inventions of a spoon-shaped tennis racquet, a synthetic soil for putting greens, and weird-shaped golf clubs never had much of an impact on play in America, his more general notions about coordination and subordination did. Children themselves became "piecework" for the play leaders, and in turn were taught to see their play as a piece of production. As "The Normal Course of Play" noted, "There is no fundamental difference between play and work."[28]

If there was to be no fundamental difference between work and play, it was because play was being transformed into the routinized, alienated experience common to industry, while industry itself was being cleansed of all play-like elements. The cult of efficiency born of scientific management was informing work and play, attempting to reduce both to a common denominator of alienation. The June 1914 issue of *The Playground* captured the essence of scientific management in its impact on play when it quoted Dr. Thomas Wood, president of the Physical Education Society of New York and professor at Teachers College, Columbia University: "The business of physical education," he said, "is to help develop a socially efficient person; a useful citizen; a good potential ancestor...."[29] The same issue carried an article by a medical doctor named Burdick. He wrote effusively about the wonders of the athletic badge test, the test which had been designed for the Public Schools Athletic League by Luther Gulick, and its relationship to scientific management. These tests called for children to pit themselves against certain predetermined standards of strength and speed in order to win a badge. But the good doctor was concerned with more than just physical achievement, as his article noted:

> The present tests correspond to the methods of scientific management. They are based on modern principles and test efficiency. At last there is standardization of effort since each boy has a measure with which he may gage his ability.
>
> Best of all, as scientific management has shown there need be no antagonism between labor and capital for both are after the same result, so, here, there will come a closer co-operation between leaders and boys. Each will help the other and our influence in the boy world will extend farther and farther as do the waves when a stone is dropped in a lake.[30]

Antidote

Both Dr. Wood and Dr. Burdick stressed the interconnectedness of play, work, and scientific management, but Hall took that connection even a step further. He saw play programs as providing a curative to industrial and social unrest. For the workers, those "who lead excessively sedentary lives [and therefore] are prone to be turbulent and extreme in both passion and opinion,"[31] he advocated a program of scientific recreation which included: (1) breaks from routine and rest for overworked organs; (2) exercise for unused faculties; and (3) elements of surprise to reawaken interest in everyday life.[32] Never mind that industrial accidents and diseases were ravaging those who sold their labor power and their families, turning the formerly healthy into half ghosts and cripples. Never mind that the inevitable counterpart of applying scientific management to work "was elimination of the elements of play that are intermingled with it."[33] These items were unavoidable costs of production for which the organized-play movement attempted to compensate through industrial recreation, evening playgrounds, social and recreation centers, etc. For the children who were learning about the horrors of industrialization at a young age either by seeing their parents at work or by working themselves,[34] and who were consequently rejecting the ethics of industrial capital by becoming revolutionaries, prostitutes, or petty thieves, play programs would provide "a wholesome outlet for youthful energy."[35]

In striving to provide a wholesome outlet, the leaders of the organized-play movement had one eye on the factory and the other on the streets, one eye on young workers and the other on children. In the factory they saw

> The day laborer of low intelligence, with a practical vocabulary of not over 500 words, who can hardly move each of his fingers without moving others or all of them, who can not move his brows or corrugate his forehead at will, and whose inflection is very monstrous.[36]

This plight they attributed to "a condition of arrest or atrophy of the later, finer, accessory system of muscles" which came about as a result of overspecialization and a concomitant lack of exercise of the large muscles. When they looked at the street, the play leaders saw these same workers protesting the injustices of capitalism:

> Make no mistake; the ordinary workingman fully understands the means which the well-to-do member of the community has of enjoying himself in automobiling, in golf, in tennis and the other modern methods of recreation.[37]

This knowledge, according to a speaker at the National Recreation Congress of 1907, would lead to "class antagonisms." Tompkins Square Park on the Lower East Side was pointed to as an example of how much positive impact an organized-play program could have on the actions and attitudes of workers. Where once "the rally to the red flag years ago always occurred here," said Seth T. Stewart, a director of the PAA "now this park is often the scene of games...and other forms of patriotic play."[38] Playgrounds like the one at

Tompkins Square were thought to have value not just as outlets for children and youth, but from at least 1907 until World War I they were valued for the role they could play with workers as deterrents to protest and as compensation for the monotony of factory piecework. As "The Normal Course of Play" noted, factory work leads to "debilitation of the body," "impairment of the mental powers," a "sense of dissatisfaction," a "pessimistic attitude toward life," and a "moral recklessness." "Such conditions" of drudgery it went on, "make slaves of men and tend inevitably toward anarchy and social unrest."[39] For men and women of power and privilege, this prospect was of no little concern; they responded accordingly.

As socialism neared its peak around 1910, the organized-play movement became more vociferous in its condemnation of factory life and more concerned with young workers as well as children. In the January 1911 issue of *The Playground*, for example, Ernest Herman wrote:

> To my mind there cannot exist anything more mind and soul destroying than modern factory piece work, —to produce hour after hour, week after week, year after year, only a very small piece of a piece.[40]

In addition to the Herman article there appeared a pamphlet by Howard Braucher, secretary of the PAA, entitled "A Life Rather than a Living";[41] a year-long campaign to raise funds and educate the public to play as a factory antidote; and suggestions by the U.S. Commission on Industrial Relations to increase playground and physical fitness programs. All these ideas, programs, and proposals were put forward with one immediate goal in mind—the strengthening of modern industrial capitalism so as to maintain the class–commodity system. And while they may have characterized production as monotonous and harmful, they never once called into question the ultimate correctness of the process. As Herman suggested, and as the leaders of the organized-play movement believed,

> We must bring back joy. The playground in its broadest conception is the only practical means of counteracting the monotonous drudgery of factory life.[42]

By counteracting the drudgery of factory life, play would enable America to go about its business, which was business. Socialism and anarchism would be consigned to their rightful places as attitudes appropriate only to certain clearly marked psychological stages of a child's development, not as viable political philosophies. Anarchism and Socialism threatened to eliminate individuality and especially competition, which was seen by Lee and by Hall as an instinct inherent to the process of developing selfhood. During what Lee called the "Big Injun Age," the child searched for self-definition through anarchy and competition. Here, games were to become "uniformly competitive ...when once they were cooperative....It is I against the world—a personality to be wrenched free and outwardly projected in the real."[43] This period was supposed to represent an evolutionary stage of humankind's development re-enacted in the child. The Big Injun Age, lasting from age six until eleven, was the third of a four-stage process of development that also included Babyhood, the Dramatic Age, and the Age of Loyalty. During the Big Injun Age the ego was thought to evolve out of the confines of cooperation and to challenge the world with a head-on audacity. During Babyhood the child was thought to move from reaching out to cling to the mother to reaching out to own and possess. The manipulative impulse of this period was, according to Lee, a time which led to "the institution of private property."[44] During the following period, the Dramatic Age, the individualistic drives for property were supposedly replaced by the craving for social solidarity. This was the age of imitation in which the child would learn the subordination of individual interests to the group through rhythm and ring games like ring-around-the-rosy. Finally, after the child passed through the Dramatic Age into the Big Injun Age where it learned to indulge its nomadism and anarchy, it passed into the Age of Loyalty where youth learned to mitigate psychosexual stress through the peer group.

Each one of these stages was thought to be useful to the child as he or she strove to achieve as aspects of his own personality the various traits developed by his evolutionary ancestors. The proper kind of play was believed to assist in the cultivation of certain of these traits and the curtailment of others less appropriate for contemporary life. As one example, Lee thought the Big Injun Age to be a period that would, if properly attended by play leaders, assist the race in "preserving the element of competition...[so that] every man [could] carve out his own life and not have it arranged for him by someone else."[45]

"Someone else" to Lee and the other leaders of the organized-play movement was a Socialist or an anarchist. Young men and women insufficiently developed through play during their formative years, they argued, were flocking to Socialism and anarchism as they experienced the degradation and exploitation of industry. Lee, Hall, Luther Gulick, and Clark Hetherington, among others, designed games and supported organizations (the Boy Scouts, for example) for the purpose of successfully competing with the lure of radical camaraderie. Lee in particular argued that boys should be involved in recreation activities specifically designed to prevent participation in radical activities on the one hand, and on the other to socialize adolescents to a specific psychology:

> There must be not merely participation in a given purpose, but participation through the fulfillment of specific function....It is true that he can lose himself very fully in the horde or mass games as in later life he may lose himself in a mob; but the point is not to lose himself, but to find the team, not to sleep, but to wake.[46]

Property

If a young man were awake, as Lee and others saw it, he would be following in the footsteps of people like Andrew Carnegie, hoisting himself up by the bootstraps, working hard and accumulating property. Property itself was considered "the backbone of personality,"[47] and represented for the play theorists the coming to consciousness of a child: "It was when man began to get clearer ideas of his own body, to distinguish between the self and the non-self, that the idea of individual ownership became possible....*mind* and self-consciousness are mutually dependent."[48] This interpretation of selfhood as possession was neither new nor limited in its impact. In a brilliant passage in *The Economic and Philosophic Manuscripts of 1844*, Marx pointed out how the bourgeoisie described possession as realization:

> The less you eat, drink and buy books; the less you go to the theater, the dance hall, the public house; the less you think, love, theorize, sing, paint, fence, etc., the more you save— the greater becomes your treasure which neither moths nor dust will devour—your *capital*. The less you *are*, the less you express your own life, the greater is your alienated life, the more you have, the greater is the store of your estranged being...and all the things which you cannot do, your money can do....it is the true endowment.[49]

As the realization of "true endowment" for the play theorists like Hall and Lee, possession meant encouraging activities that fostered a worship of things, which ultimately led to alienation between children. The prize, whether it was a camera or movie tickets or sweets, came to take on a life of its own sometimes more important to the luxury-starved children than their own peers. More than one playground report, in fact, cautioned about the overzealousness that awarding prizes engendered, and more than once were competitors jeered and booed as a way of breaking their concentration and improving the chances of "favorites." These antagonisms erupted not only when the object of reward was a valuable prize, but even when prizes were as valueless as buttons or badges. Children who were pitted against one another in pursuit of objects purposely made scarce sometimes acted with all the ill manners and tenacity of a J. P. Morgan determined to make more money.

Although the play theorists argued that property was "an instrument to avert pain and procure pleasure,"[50] the very fact that property was held as a commodity and privatized made it the exact opposite. Emma Goldman noted this in an article entitled "Too Little Joy" which appeared in the anarchist journal *Mother Earth* in 1908. There she pointed out and condemned the fact that joy is held as a scarce commodity and "that there is not enough to go around." Joy, she noted, had been turned into, "greed" and "love into lust" by the capitalists and their minions.[51]

Aside from the tournaments, games of competition, and the extirpation of fantasy by prepackaged stories like those of Sir Walter Scott and *Cinderella** (all of which have been discussed in other chapters) there were the Penny Provident Funds which concerned themselves with "money training." Money training was an idea developed by Jacob Abbott as early as 1874 and incorporated as part of settlement house work at the turn of the century. According to a report by the Neighborhood Guild Branch of the University Settlement:

> The system involves the depositing of small coins by the children, and the pasting of stamps, designating the amount on their pasteboard cards, or bankbooks as they are called by the workers.[52]

The most frequent deposits were five and ten cents; the average account totaled $1.58; and the maximum withdrawal was fifty cents, as stipulated by the fund.[53] The Puritan/political-economist values of thrift and mathematized experience ruled as Penny Provident Funds became models "of the financial world in the home [settlement] with the mother [social worker] playing the banker and the child the businessman."[54] The acquisitive instinct or the "receptacle habit," as Lee called it, was thus duly served.

Delinquency

If property was to be the backbone of personality and the love of money was to be inculcated in the immigrant children, then it followed that some children would pursue wealth with such zeal that they would overstep the bounds of legality in pursuit of possessions. But while the theories of Hall and Lee might allow for expression of "natural instincts" such as truancy or running away during the Big Injun Age, when it came to adolescence and property rights, the foul line was clearly drawn. In *Play in Education* Lee made this point clear: "In a civilized community law

---

*Lee described literature as "a mold into which the child's life in the imagination may be run." [Joseph Lee, *Play in Education* (Washington, D.C.: McGrath, 1915), p. 315].

and order must be upheld. Life could not go on if no man's property were safe from wanton injury and depredation." Although the task of repression was not the primary function of the play movement, Lee and the others stressed that intervention *was* necessary because, as he put it: "If the boy does not learn the existence and solidity of social institutions now, when he is a boy, he never will."[55] Repression was certainly not ignored, but coercion as a technique of control was something more appropriately left to police, courts, and probation officers. The organized-play movement was to provide the other side of the control dialectic, adaptation, or as Lee called it, "guidance."

Because crime and property are such vital concerns of the bourgeoisie, the idea of guiding children with and through play as a prophylactic for delinquency was enthusiastically received by the growing middle class. "Playgrounds curb crime!" was the advertising slogan that helped gain public support for the organized-play movement. The PAA played on this concern for law and order and economy by advertising the savings in reform school and prison budgets that could be realized through the building of playgrounds.

Play guidance was considered extremely important because

> the whole question of juvenile law-breaking—or at least 9/10ths of it—is thus a question of children's play. A child who breaks the law is, in nine cases out of ten, not a criminal. He is obeying an instinct that is not only legitimate but vital.[56]

In order that this instinct be realized in a more acceptable way, the child was to be taught the Athlete's Code of Honor, which would give him a conception of citizenship and duty, that the policemen were friends who wanted the children to get as much play as they could, and to use the playground and its games as ways of giving vent to those pent-up energies. Whether Lee, Hall, Gulick, or the others really believed that the provision of guidance and play facilities would actually decrease the number of juvenile delinquents, or whether they used the delinquency arguments as a red herring to gather public support, as historian Dom Cavallo argues, is a moot point. Certainly, there was a paucity of material or data other than "opinion" that substantiated their arguments that playgrounds reduced crime, and there was a tremendous public relations effort on the part of the reformers to frighten the public about juvenile delinquency and simultaneously offer the curative of playgrounds. But the point is that they *did* argue and attempt to substantiate a link between criminal behavior among juveniles and a lack of supervised play facilities. The reduction of delinquency was listed as the number two item on the PAA creed; many of the propaganda pictures used for fundraising had pictures of children on a playground or play street with a police officer prominent in the foreground; and many of the quotes solicited and run in newspapers and posted in the playgrounds, attributed to famous people, noted the control of delinquency as at least one positive benefit to be derived from organized-play programs. In New York City, even the Children's Court cited "the normal instinct for play" as the motivating force behind a great many of the acts which brought juveniles into its presence.[57] Given the breadth of the effort to link play with delinquency, we must investigate the claim that lack of play made for crime and that someone sneaking on the cop as a boy would not "hesitate to play the same game on a larger scale...when he comes to be a man."[58]

The Burns Study

At the Second Annual National Recreation Congress, held in Chicago in 1908, Allen Burns, dean of the Chicago School of Civics and Philanthropy, delivered a paper titled "The Relation of Playground to Juvenile Delinquency." His thesis was that

> The presence of parks and playgrounds in a neighborhood is coincident with a decrease in the numbers of cases of juvenile delinquency and with an increase in the proportion of cases successfully cared for by the Court.[59]

In order to test this hypothesis, Burns studied data furnished by all cases brought into the Juvenile Court of Chicago during the first eight years of its history, the period from July 1899 to June 1907. This information was used to construct a map of the city onto which tacks indicating the block from which the delinquent came were placed. The map included areas that had been set aside by the Chicago playground authorities for use as parks and playgrounds. According to Burns, "By this device it was possible to determine exactly the distribution of juvenile delinquency and the geographical relation, at least, between juvenile delinquency and playgrounds."[60] This study of what one might call the "geography of delinquency" was a constant point of reference for all the major playground advocates over the next decade. "The Chicago data indicate," "A study of juvenile delinquency in the Midwest shows"—phrases like these dot the speeches of people like Lee, Jane Addams, William Maxwell (New York superintendent of schools), and others. It is also worth noting that the study was funded by the Russell Sage Foundation, and that immediately after the congress and the report dispatched by its representative, Lawrence Veiller, the foundation became *the major* financial support of the fledgling PAA in its first few years.

Burns's work was a prime example of an unholy marriage consummated at the turn of the century between social science and juvenile control. This union, according to sociologist Alexander Liazos, has existed throughout the century, during which time "social work, psychology, and social sciences techniques have been used to socialize the boys and girls into a 'realistic' acceptance of their place in society." This place for "children of the poor, working class, and minority groups," against whom most juvenile delinquency prevention programs were and are aimed, is "the bottom of the social and occupational worlds. Especially for the boys, this has meant socializing them to fit into low-level, unskilled or semi-skilled jobs with few making it to higher jobs and positions so as to perpetuate the belief that anybody can make it if they work hard enough."[61] Ideology thus ruled science, and Burns's study suffered accordingly. Among the problems with Burns's study are: (1) the unreliability of his statistical base; (2) contradictions within his own findings; and (3) a failure to consider alternative variables. Briefly, each of these errors is treated below.

Statistics

The problem with Burns's statistics began at his beginning. First, he failed to consider all those cases of juvenile delinquency that never came before the court. Given the findings of recent studies in self-reported crime, this population is usually taken as at least twice the formal arrest and arraignment rate. Second, of those that did come before the court's jurisdiction, only 90 percent of the delinquents' residences were plotted. Burns claimed that in order to use maps that were of scale and "practicable for use," 10 percent of the residents had to be left out.[62] This of course means that those delinquents were from outside the most predominant locations plotted and studied, suggesting that they might be of a different class. Even if that supposition is incorrect, it is important to note that the figure of 10 percent could be crucial in determining the degree of significance. Finally, because Burns provided no raw scores in his report, we never know to what extent his results are statistically valid and/or to what degree.

Contradictions

Burns concluded that with large parks, "it is impossible to say how much such parks account for the scarcity of juvenile delinquency in their neighborhood"[63] because they were situated in affluent sections of the city. Regarding municipal playgrounds, he concluded that "these playgrounds have had at least no appreciable immediate effect upon the juvenile delinquency within their possible radii of efficiency."[64] Only in reference to the small parks of Chicago's South Side does he find any connection between a decrease of juvenile crime and the provision of play facilities. He claimed that "after the small parks had been operating for two years, the South Side alone showed a decrease in delinquency of 17 percent relative to the delinquency of the whole city, while the whole city had increased its delinquency 12 percent, a showing in favor of the South Side of a difference of 29 percent."[65] But within some of the subdistricts of the South Side (probation districts), the delinquency rates varied and in one instance (District 9) there was an inverse relationship between the accessibility of small parks and delinquency rates. Burns's figures and his contention that small parks are an important factor in decreasing juvenile delinquency are further marred because the population in the neighborhoods with small parks was constantly changing and this mandated a change in court procedures, the court giving "additional attention" to those neighborhoods in flux.[66] It was where there were stable populations (probably indicating steady employment opportunities and perhaps even a living wage) that the greatest reduction of delinquency occurred.

Alternative Variables

Given all the difficulties mentioned above it seems redundant to point to yet another set of problems within this study, but because juvenile delinquency prevention programs have continued to perpetuate the myth that sports facilities decreased crime, almost magically by their very presence, additional critique is necessary. One major point to be made is that Burns never considered changes in the age group covered by the juvenile courts. Hence, a decrease of delinquency in a certain area may very well be the result of a decrease in the number of people who fall under the legal heading of delinquents (in Chicago during this period it was age sixteen and under). Another factor ignored by Burns is that since over 22 percent of the cases that came before the court were for such crimes as disorderly conduct and malicious mischief, and that since these "crimes" often involved violation of laws that prohibited ball playing in the street, the establishment of a park where children could play would have absolutely no effect on the children's behavior but rather indicated a change in police procedures. Instead of arresting children for playing ball, cops would encourage it. Although it is true that the location changed, which served the needs of law and order in many important ways (traffic flow was increased, commerce advanced, children were socialized to compartmentalized experiences, etc.), in reality there was a wholesale redefinition of the law.

During the first decade of the Chicago Juvenile Court (1899–1909), 80 percent of the children brought before the court were poor and working-class children. Over 50 percent of the alleged offenses of the boys were stealing, while the girls were similarly charged with stealing as their major offense. Incorrigibility made up the next major charge for boys (21.7 percent) and "immorality" was next highest for the girls at 31.4 percent. When disorderly conduct (16.2 percent)* and malicious mischief (6.5 percent)*[67] are considered, there appears a pattern of behavior, or rather a pattern of repression of certain types of behavior, that is clearly class based. In New York City, similar figures reveal a consistent policy on the part of the police (coercion dialectic) which places the activities of play reformers (adaptation dialectic) and children in a class perspective. When delinquency prevention and control are considered in conjunction with the industrial work of the playground and the effort to socialize certain class-based values into working-class children, the purpose of such programs becomes crystal clear: to get "the children of the poorer classes to accept dead-end jobs, to reduce the rate of crime and recidivism, and to keep them quiet."[68] Burns's study was a pseudoscientific attempt to legitimize the newly evolving efforts of social workers and social scientists; his class position almost precluded any alternative finding. His inability to recognize both the methodological and conceptual problems in his work stem from his assumptions about life and society, and his tacit acceptance of information put forth by institutions such as the police and the courts. Because he failed to see and compensate for their class functions as institutions serving the perpetuation of the status quo, Burns wound up performing merely an ideological rather than a scientific role. Because his study resonated with the sounds that the play reformers wanted to hear, it was

---

*Figures for boys only.

hailed and used as proof of the importance of playgrounds across the nation. "Playgrounds curb crime!" became an advertising slogan that helped gain middle- and upper-middle-class support for the organized-play movement. The PAA even went so far as to publish the savings in reform school, prison, and other corrections budgets that could be realized through building playgrounds, which were cheaper.

The real truth about crime was more aptly expressed by people like Emma Goldman and Benzion Liber. Goldman noted with sarcasm the tremendous concern of police for craps shooting or card playing by children and adults while such behavior was only an "insignificant part of that great gambling conspiracy known as capitalism."[69] Liber, for his part, could not help but reflect on how ridiculous it was to teach a child not to kill, but yet sanction war; to teach a child not to steal, yet hold up legal (industrial) robbery as "a model for emulation." He urged a "rational education" which would allow free course to the child's questions and "perhaps the child would then discover how deeply immoral and corrupt society is, perhaps he would find out the true meaning of commerce, of capital, of war, of charity, of riches, of inheritance."[70] Perhaps. But one thing is for sure; that kind of education would never come from the playgrounds.

What did come from the playgrounds was a concern for property rights and propriety. The prose of the factory spread and invaded the art of sport, forcing children to confront alienation as natural. With the degradation of labor, the artistry of sport became as mundane as a Gillette Blue Blades commercial. Colonized sport became the reality principle imposed on a playful spirit which had formerly been an autonomous sphere of working-class culture. The street games of children, formerly realms of fantasy and flight, were subverted and replaced by games which were models of a reality in which possession as selfhood ruled. Just as the assault on the pushcart was to teach the child to approach the marketplace in neatly compartmentalized categories (pharmacies, food stores, millineries, and other specialty shops instead of peddlers and pushcarts laden with pins, pots, elixirs, and potions), so too were work and play to be compartmentalized. The child's very growth was seen by Hall, Lee et al., as little more than a series of bracketed stages within which some behaviors were acceptable and to be encouraged, while others were to be squelched. As social historian Stanley Aronowitz has noted, work became divested of its playful elements while play was proposed as its compensation for the suffering that playless work entails. Of course, in the strange world ruled by commodities no activity is immune to penetration by the marketplace mentality. What we have tried to show in this chapter is that play/sport/games were certainly no exceptions. Theories were developed, scientific studies undertaken, and policies established that had the effect of casting a net over childhood for the Jewish working class and drawing them more tightly under the reign of capital.

In degrading spontaneous, free activity to a means, estranged labor makes man's species life a means to his physical existence.

—Karl Marx
The Economic and Philosophic Manuscripts of 1844

Endgame

The struggle of the Jewish working class* against the colonization and commoditization of everyday life was not the first such battle, but it was the first within which the question of leisure and the dynamics of play took on such a grave importance. Since the industrial revolution sports have been an arena wherein the worker might transcend the barbarism of commodity relationships. In *The Economic and Philosophic Manuscripts of 1844*, Marx writes that under capitalism the worker is "depressed spiritually and physically to the condition of a machine and from being a man becomes an abstract activity and a belly." As a result of this loss of self, the worker "feels himself freely active in his animal functions—eating, drinking, procreating or at most in his dwelling and in his dressing-up, etc."[1] I interpret "dressing up" in the way that Huizinga uses it in *Homo Ludens*,[2] as a characteristic of play and sport. Thus, in addition to being an escape sport becomes a place where-

---

*This book has focused on the rise of organized play and the destruction of immigrant street culture on the Lower East Side of New York City during the period 1890-1914. Although it concentrates explicitly on the Jewish community that lived on the Lower East Side, the implications drawn from this population and the ramifications of the rise of organized play extend far beyond the confines of this time, space, and ethnic group.

in the worker might "affirm himself" and "develop freely his physical and mental energy."[3] As C. L. R. James has shown, sport provided an emotive vehicle by which Trinidadians were able to understand for themselves that the colonial British were no better than they themselves were and this was a powerful impetus for the independence movement.[4] In the middle and late nineteenth century, at a time when political economy was articulating and informing the ideology of the bourgeoisie "by counting the lowest level of life (existence) as the general standard," workers were rejecting a philosophy which "spares man the need of either fresh air or exercise."[5] They were playing at track meets, Turnfests, baseball, rock on dock—in streets, alleys, and fields everywhere. As it became impossible for the ruling class to restrict enjoyment to themselves, play/sport was colonized. It was transformed from an autonomous cultural activity of workers where their own definitions of and attitudes toward time, space, and mobility (property, work, and social relationships) ruled, to a mechanism for the efficient transmission of capitalist values.

The process began in the late 1880s with the founding and growth of a series of normal schools for physical education organized by the YMCA (1886), Chautauqua (1888), and the Boston Normal School (1889). These schools and their ideologies served as a training ground for thousands of play leaders and physical educators. Needless to say, they were not without a class character. Admission to any of them required a high school education, character and family background checks, and a physical examination. The curricula, which included marching tactics, voice training, aesthetic dancing for women, sports, and biology, were shaped by those institutions and people who had formed the Association for Advancement of Physical Education in 1885.[6]

The AAPE had been established as an amalgam of every existing group and system of physical culture *except* the Turners and the Turnvereins. This influenced the subsequent determination of both the form and content of sports and play in America. The Turners were in turn Free Soilers, Abolitionists, Socialists, and Communists. They stood clearly at the forefront of labor–capital struggles on the side of labor in contradistinction to the elite athletic clubs and middle-class Ys.[7] Perhaps more important, their system of gymnastics and physical culture was one of "harmonious activity and cooperation of both mind and body." It was "general physical culture and not the culture of one special branch. Therefore it declined the development of a certain organ or faculty at the expense of others."[8] In short, it was a system which contravened the specialization and subdivision of the human being through exercise, and therefore it was a system uniquely and innately critical of the capitalist mode of human reproduction. The idea of an integrated mind and body with a material base in a system that strove for all-around physical development which relied on music as the mode of synchronization rather than the voice of a "leader" (as did, for example, the Swedish system which partially supplanted the German–Turner gymnastics) was, consciously or not, anathema to physical educators drawn from the elite of American society.

The late nineteenth and early twentieth centuries were times when conception was being separated from execution in the productive act in the capitalist mode of production. These were the times of Taylorism, and there was an extremely smooth meshing between the AAPE form of physical education and Taylorism, described by Braverman in *Labor and Monopoly Capital* as a system which "raised the concept of control to an entirely new plane." Taylor "asserted as an absolute necessity for adequate management, the dictation to the worker of the precise manner in which work is to be performed."[9] This strategy was reflected in the new organization and practices of physical education. As the factory was becoming an arena of estrangement and alienation and as the productive process shifted from workers to managers, so too did the technology of physical culture pass from the working class to a group of upper- and middle-class educators. The synchronization of mind and body was destroyed and supplanted by a system of muscular specialization and hierarchy.

The people responsible for the shift from physical *cul-*

ture, wherein the body is treated as a totality, to physical *education,* where the body becomes one means toward different ends, were the AAPE leaders who became patriarchs of the playground and scholastic sports movement of the first two decades of the twentieth century. In his *The Making of American Physical Education,* Arthur Weston credits AAPE leaders such as Luther Gulick, Clark Hetherington, and Thomas Wood with breaking "with the traditions of formal gymnastics and [giving] shape and content to a distinctively twentieth century program of physical education, which centers upon the physical as an arena for promoting education." This, according to Weston, contrasted with the prevailing view "that the physical body should be developed as an end in itself."[10]

This move by early physical education ideologies away from the Turner–German gymnastics system, first to the Swedish system (emphasizing posture, concentration on the respiratory organs, and concern with the nervous system as opposed to muscular development) and later to the institutionalization of games/play/sports as the mode of physical development, had grave consequences. It involved the transformation of the body from an end in itself to a means—of education, morality, societal integration. This ideological shift was a factor in alienating the worker from his/her body, and thereby fostering false consciousness. In the last move, from exercise to games, the physical demands of the body are subsumed in the ethos of competition with its attendant social perversions, viz. hierarchy, overspecialization, and repressed sexuality. At the workplace and in the nonwork hours, the laborer is reduced to less than what he/she might fully be in the individual species self, and

> becomes ever more dependent on every fluctuation in market price, on the application of capital, and on the whim of the rich.[11]

The shift in consciousness away from the body as purpose and toward heuristic play reflects and reinforces the shift at the workplace from craft and artisan production for a home and market economy to one in which the entire tenor of the process is controlled by management exclusively for the marketplace. This move is one in which the first two principles of the process are: "gathering and the development of knowledge of labor processes, and...the concentration of this knowledge as the exclusive province of management—together with its essential converse, the absence of such knowledge among the workers."[12] The third principle, the use of such knowledge as a tool of exploitation directed at the workers, we have seen in the rise of institutionalized play and sports through the 1890s and more saliently in the first two decades of the twentieth century.

Through the establishment of playgrounds where trained directors formalized play, institutionalized hierarchy, legitimized external control and rewards, and mandated repressed sexuality, the elite was able to "Americanize" the immigrants and teach them such attitudes as would be beneficial toward maintaining the status quo. The *shtetl* and Lower East Side games of low organization and minimum role differentiation, which were sometimes coed and within which action had not become reified into positions but was rather a part of style form and skill—these games gave way to playground games which were to be vehicles for and symbols of the American Way of Life. Teams were set, boys and girls were separated, winners were given material rewards, and everything was organized by the play leader and the clock. Whereas the games of the street had been part of the social fabric of the community—with pushcarts, for example, serving as "base" for games of tag— the new games were isolated, abstracted, set apart, and fenced off. This separation accomplished three things: first, removal of the games from the street opened the streets up to traffic, thus making commerce faster and easier; second, removal of the games from the street eliminated the vast crowds which gathered to watch the games and which were often mobilized as protesters; finally, removal of the games from the street meant the removal of the child from the street—no longer would children be able to learn about sex, poverty, unemployment, and strikes from the people on the street around them. Children would go to school and from there to the playground. From the playground they would head home for a night of homework, and in the process they would be shielded (or so the reformers hoped) from the harshness, immorality, and radicalism of the street milieu. They would grow to adulthood as hard-working, respectful Americans, not as foreigners or political malcontents.

The colonization of sport and play revealed a calculation and efficiency that did eventually overwhelm the working class immigrants. Elaborate theories were developed that justified the programs offered by the organized-play movement; and the Socialists and anarchists, although they at times understood the importance of play, were too busy fighting on the political and economic fronts to pay much attention to the dynamics of childhood/sport/ideology. The schematization of working-class experience which had previously been done by those who were a part of or aligned with that class (sweatshop poets, cafe intellectuals, etc.) was forfeited to those whose interests were diametrically opposed to the objective and subjective needs of the proletariat. From an early age onward, as we have seen, children received conscious and unconscious, formal and informal messages about strikes, Socialism, work, sexuality, and patriotism from the organized-play movement leaders that flew in the face of their class consciousness. Citizenship, upward mobility, and monogamy all became desires of great value, replacing revolutionary social values as American capitalism grew to maturity, extending beyond the world of work and ever more so into the world of play. More and more play became, like work, a production rather than a process. All that was left was for capitalism to commoditize the sports experience, to interpose money between humans and their natural propensity for sport, play, or exercise. This came with the rise of spectator sports in the 1920s.

Once sport had been alienated from the control of the community, it was sold back to the immigrants and the entire working class. The 1920s were the Golden Age of Sports, marked by the construction of municipal stadia, radio broadcasts of college and professional games, and the institutionalization of the sports section of the city newspapers. As the all-American running back Red Grange brought financial success to the National Football League, as the legendary Babe Ruth built his home in the Bronx, and as boxing and racing drew millions to rings and tracks nationally, participation turned to spectatorship.[13] The National Amateur Athletic Federation estimated that participation in sandlot baseball, for example, had fallen off by 50 percent from 1923 to 1925.[14] College football had grown to a multimillion-dollar enterprise and could no longer "afford" loosely run, student-controlled teams where involvement was the key. Professional coaching staffs scouted and scoured near and far every potential box office star. As Marx wrote, money came to assert itself as "the alienated ability of mankind turning man's powers into their contrary."[15] In the 1920s it transformed the physical body from the active to the passive, the working class from sports producers to consumers, and it made the potentially transcendent experience of sports a mere mundane companion of Rheingold and a rocking chair.

Like any art form, mechanical reproduction of sport through the press, radio, and television, violated its authenticity by removing it from the time and space of its creation. The tradition, history, and aura of originality and uniqueness that is integral to the sports experience as phenomenon or folklore was shattered by the accessibility provided by mass spectatorism and electronic transmission. Sport and play as autonomous realms of creativity and expression for the working class succumbed to the pressure of statistics, which asserts the universal equality of all things. The result is their condemnation to the world of manipulated pseudo-satisfaction.

Truly, a dialectic still exists as people adapt mass culture to their own needs and transform some of the more alienating and fragmented experiences into opportunities for self-realization, community, and control. When a worker bets against the smart money or the odds, surely it is a much more important act than the mere hunger for accumulation asserting itself. Such a bettor is claiming that his (or her) own knowledge or information is better than that of the expert (read power structure). That bettor is announcing a belief in his/her own capabilities despite the definition of the situation provided by the power structure. When a group of people gathers around a television to watch Sunday baseball or football, the sense of community created is perhaps no more incidental to the experience than the game itself. Mass culture is not a net without pores or even holes—there is struggle—but the overwhelming reality is one of oppression, alienation, and hegemony.

Unanswered Questions and New Directions

We are now at a critical juncture not unlike the critical period of the turn of the century when a new leisure-time phenomenon burst into American culture as organized play. Today, a mass sports movement of participation and self-realization has sprung up among variegated segments of the population. This movement is nondialectically hailed by some as innately progressive. I want to call attention to the strategic and theoretical errors that are involved in nonreflective endorsement of "involvement" for, as we have seen in the rise of organized play, involvement can become an abstraction that lends itself to forms of alienation and exploitation similar to those of spectatorship.

As the crisis of capitalism deepens and corporations seek new ways to mold the hearts and minds of the masses, sports participation becomes a very lucrative avenue of investment. Today, multinationals like Pepsi, Coke, MacDonald's, Bristol-Myers, and many others are literally falling all over each other in an attempt to play ball with the people. Their sponsorship of tournaments, leagues, events, and summer programs which come into contact with millions of youngsters and adults alike is the newest form of alienation. As the latest and last report by the President's Commission on Olympic Sports asserts: "The United States must rely on its greatest strength, free enterprise, to help finance amateur sport." Marketing penetration plans are being developed and sports goals are being matched in the interest of benefiting the corporation by "building credibility among youth reducing the [employee] turnover rate" and developing new forms of cultural imperialism where the worker would identify with a corporation-sponsored athlete and thereby any "potential labor problems are worked out beforehand."[16] This corporate colonization of sports on a participatory basis, now sanctioned by a presidential commission, is nothing short of social lobotomy. For those social scientists, critical theorists, and athletes concerned with the future of sport, the task ahead is to debunk the myth of participation as salvation and at the same time articulate a philosophy of praxis which provides a framework for the realization of mind and body, self and society.

The legacy of repressed/sublimated sexuality, atomized leisure, and homogenized play forms developed during the rise of organized play are still with us and are now taking on new forms thanks to the multinationals which have built upon the 'legacy' left by Lee, Hall, Schiff, and others. The denial of physical expression, or the alienation of sports, is something the working-class person feels every minute of every day. She/he creates an ever-more-powerful world of objects that lessen her/his power. "So much does labor's realization appear as a loss of realization that the worker loses realization to the point of starving to death"[17]—or obesity. In play, sport, and exercise one produces, but the product is a new body that does not realize itself as an alien object that faces and lessens the creator. The product *is* the creator/worker: through play or sport one comes to understand experientially that the body is not a thing—it is a situation, a force of history. Thus, playing is a political act which affirms the reality of humans as creative, conscious beings who can and must extend this phenomenon of self-realization outward to the totality. Ultimately, this will mean a society of neither playgrounds, nor Pepsi tournaments, nor even athletes, but rather one of people who engage in athletics, among other things.

Notes

Introduction

1. Elias Tcherikower, *The Early Jewish Movement in the U.S.* (New York: YIVO, 1961), chap. 4.

2. Ibid., chap. 6.

3. Seymour Joseph, *Jewish Immigration to the U.S. 1881–1910* (New York: Columbia University, 1914), chap. 2.

4. Werner Keller, *Diaspora* (New York: Harcourt Brace and World, 1969) p. 469.

5. Soja Szajkowski, "The Attitude of American Jews to Eastern European Jewish Immigration," *Publications of the American Jewish Historical Society* 40, no. 3 (March 1951): 221.

6. For this entire discussion of the Yiddish theater, see Howe, *World of Our Fathers* (New York: Harcourt Brace Jovanovich, 1976), pp. 463–92.

7. Mordecai Soltes, *The Yiddish Press: An Americanizing Agency* (New York: Teachers College Press, 1925), p. 24.

8. *The Worker*, August 30, 1903.

9. Samuel Chotzinoff, *A Lost Paradise* (New York: Knopf, 1955), pp. 137–38.

10. Author's interview of Ben Levine, Summer 1976.

11. Howe, *World of Our Fathers*, p. 235.

12. Harry Roskolenko, *The Time That Was Then* (New York: Dial, 1971), p. 185.

13. Bella Mead, "The Social Pleasures of the East Side Jews" (M.A. thesis, Columbia University, 1904), p. 5.

14. "Annual Report 1899," University Settlement, New York, New York, p. 23.

15. Author's interview of Lilian Skupsky, Summer 1976.

Chapter 1

1. Edwin T. Christmae, quoted in the *New York Times*, April 29, 1896, p. 12.

2. Ibid., April 24, 1896, p. 4.

3. Ibid., February 2, 1894, p. 9.

4. Edward P. North, "Asphalt for the Poor," ibid., May 30, 1895, p. 16.

5. Ibid.

6. *New York Times*, April 29, 1895, p. 12.

7. Editorial, ibid., May 30, 1895, p. 4.

8. Jacob Riis, *The Battle with the Slum* (New York, 1900), pp. 140–41, quoted in Thomas Brown, "The Movement for Publicly Financed Playgrounds in New York, 1890-1903" (M.A. thesis, Columbia University, 1976), p. 25.

9. "Annual Report 1899," University Settlement, New York, New York, pp. 22-3.

10. Samuel Chotzinoff, *A Lost Paradise* (New York: Knopf, 1955), pp. 88–89.

11. Harry Roskolenko, *The Time That Was Then* (New York: Dial Press, 1971), p. 24.

12. Author's interview of Clara Hooper, Summer 1976.

13. Author's interview of Morris Mikelbank.

14. Douglas Kerr, "Culture and the Street" (M.A. thesis, Columbia University, 1974), p. 22.

15. Author's interview of Ben Levine, Summer 1976.

16. Chotzinoff, *Lost Paradise*, p. 85.

17. *New York Times*, October 12, 1894, p. 1; ibid., October 13, 1894, p. 5; ibid., October 14, 1894, p. 8.

18. Eddie Cantor, *My Life Is in Your Hands* (New York: Curtis Publishing Co., 1928), pp. 27–28.

19. George Waring, quoted in the *New York Times*, March 3, 1896, p. 11.

20. Editorial, *New York Times*, May 11, 1902, p. 8.

21. "Annual Report 1900," University Settlement, New York, New York, p. 30.

22. G. Stanley Hall, "The Question of Coeducation," *Munsey's Magazine* 34, no. 5 (February 1906): 591.

23. Roskolenko, *Time That Was*, p. 98.

24. Irving Howe, *World of Our Fathers* (New York: Harcourt Brace Jovanovich, 1970), p. 256.

25. The People's Institute of New York, "The City Where Crime Is Play: Appendix" (January 1914), p. 44, quoted in the *New York Times*, July 5, 1914, p. 9.

26. Author's interview of Charles Stein, Summer 1976.

27. *New York Times*, November 6, 1894, p. 9.

28. Melech Epstein, *Jewish Labor in the U.S.A.* (New York: KTAV, 1969), 1:384.

29. Quoted in Roskolenko, *Time That Was*, pp. 73, 78.

30. Cf. Jane Jacobs, *The Life and Death of Great American Cities* (New York: Random House, 1961).

31. Theodore Roosevelt, quoted in *The Playground* 1, no. 1 (April 1907): p. 3.

32. Playground Association of America, pamphlet #32, p. 4.

33. Ibid., #26, p. 1.

34. Playground Association of America, "A Suggestion to the Millionaire," *The Playground* 1, no. 2 (May 1907): 8.

35. "Annual Report 1909," New York City Children's Court, pp. 13–14. In addition to appearances before the court, children (or their families) could be fined ten dollars for every offense.

36. Joseph Lee, "Play as an Antidote to Civilization," Playground Association of America pamphlet #89, pp. 12–13.

37. Playground Association of America, "The Normal Course of Play," in *Proceedings of the Third National Recreation Congress*, 1909, p. 124.

38. John C. Chase, "Street Games of New York City," *The Pedagogical Seminary* 12, (1905), p. 504.

39. "Annual Report 1910," New York Parks and Playgrounds Association, p. 13.

40. The People's Institute of New York, "The City Where," p. 44.

Chapter 2

1. Author's interview of Isidore Kanowitz, Summer 1976.

2. Joseph Lee, *Constructive and Preventive Philanthropy* (Norwood, Massachusetts: Macmillan Co., 1902), p. 123.

3. Idem, *Play in Education* (Washington, D.C.: McGrath, 1915), p. viii.

4. Cf. David L. Miller, *Gods and Games* (New York: Harper and Row, 1973).

5. Herbert Marcuse, *Eros and Civilization* (New York: Vintage, 1955), p. 178.

6. Antonio Gramsci, *Prison Notebooks* (New York: International Publishers, 1971), p. 12.

7. Cf. Richard Lichtman, "Marx's Theory of Ideology," *Socialist Revolution* 5, no. 1.

8. *New York Times*, May 30, 1895, p. 13.

9. *Age of Steel*, August 5, 1882, quoted in Herbert Gutman, *Work, Culture and Society in Industrializing America* (New York: Knopf, 1976), p. 39.

10. "Souvenir Book of 1895 Fair" (New York: Educational Alliance, 1895), p. 23.

11. Howard Braucher, "A Year's Growth in the Play Movement 1911–12" (address to the Playground Congress of 1912), pp. 9–10.

12. Roy Lubove, *The Progressives and the Slums* (Pittsburgh: University of Pittsburgh Press, 1962), p. 188.

13. David B. Tyack, *The One Best System* (Cambridge, Mass.: Harvard University Press, 1974), pp. 40–50.

14. Eddie Cantor, *My Life Is in Your Hands* (New York: Curtis Publishing Co., 1928), p. 30.

15. Allen Davis, *Spearheads for Reform: The Social Settlements and the*

Progressive Movement 1890-1914 (New York: Oxford University Press, 1967), p. 41.

16. Cantor, *My Life*, pp. 33-34.

17. Wilhelm Reich, *Sex-Pol Essays 1929-1934* (New York: Vintage, 1972), p. 309.

18. James B. Reynolds, quoted in "Annual Report 1900," University Settlement Society, New York, New York, p. 14.

19. George Lukacs, *History and Class Consciousness* (Cambridge, Mass.: MIT Press, 1975), p. 69.

20. James Weinstein, *The Corporate Ideal in the Liberal State 1900-18* (Boston: Beacon Press, 1968), chap. 3.

21. Alan Nevins and John Krout, *The Greater City 1898-1948* (New York: Columbia University Press, 1948), p. 125.

22. "Report on the Vacation Schools and Playgrounds, of the Department of Education of the City of New York," 1900, p. 43.

23. Robert H. Weibe, *The Search for Order 1877-1920* (New York: Hill and Wang, 1967), p. 169.

24. "Annual Report 1898," University Settlement, New York, New York.

25. Jacob Riis, *Children of the Tenements* (New York: Macmillan Co., 1903), p. 1.

Chapter 3

1. Charles McCarthy, quoted in James Weinstein, *The Corporate Ideal in the Liberal State 1900-18* (Boston: Beacon Press, 1968), p. 202.

2. Richard F. Knapp, "Parks and Politics: The Rise of Municipal Responsibility for Playgrounds in New York City 1887-1905" (M.A. thesis, Duke University, 1968), p. 64.

3. N. Janssen Rose, quoted in ibid., pp. 60-65.

4. A total of $3 million was at issue.

5. Walter Vrooman, quoted in Knapp, "Parks and Politics," p. 64.

6. Ibid., pp. 60-65.

7. *Laws of New York*, 111th sess. (1888), quoted in ibid., p. 61.

8. "First Annual Report," New York Society for Parks and Playgrounds for Children, January 1893, p. 10.

9. Richard Hofstadter, *The Age of Reform* (New York: Knopf, 1956), p. 213.

10. Cf. S. P. Rudens, "A Half Century of Community Service: The Story of the New York Educational Alliance," *American Jewish Yearbook* 46 (1944-45).

11. Louis Marshall, "Statement to the Commission on Immigration and Naturalization of the House of Representatives," *American Jewish Yearbook* 12 (1910-11): 38.

12. Rudens, "A Half Century," p. 77.

13. *New York Times*, November 30, 1900, p. 6.

14. *Educational Alliance*, microfilm roll 2 (1909). YIVO Collection, New York City.

15. "Annual Report 1902," Educational Alliance, New York, New York, p. 21.

16. *Educational Alliance*, microfilm roll 4 (October 28, 1919). YIVO Collection, New York City.

17. "Souvenir Book of 1895 Fair" (New York: Educational Alliance, 1895), p. 23.

18. Author's interview of Charles Stein, Summer 1976.

19. Bernarr MacFadden, *Physical Culture*, August 1904, p. 153.

20. A. H. Fromerson, "The Years of Immigrant Adjustment," *Proceedings of the National Conference of Jewish Charities* 3 (1904): 120-21.

21. Allen Davis, *Spearheads for Reform: The Social Settlements and the Progressive Movement 1890-1914* (New York: Oxford University Press, 1967), p. 8.

22. Ibid., p. 138.

23. Jacob Riis, *How the Other Half Lives* (New York: Hill and Wang, 1957), p. 51.

24. Ibid., p. 11.

25. Roy Lubove, *The Progressives and the Slums* (Pittsburgh: University of Pittsburgh Press, 1962), pp. 91-92.

26. Ibid., p. 99.

27. Richard Watson Gilder, Letter to the Editor, *New York Times*, January 24, 1895, p. 3.

28. *New York Times*, January 17, 1896, p. 5.

29. Cf. Knapp, "Parks and Politics."

30. "Report of the Committee on Small Parks of the City of New York, 1897," p. 2.

31. "Outdoor Recreation League," Box 14. J. G. Phelps Stokes Collection, Columbia University, New York City.

32. *New York Times*, October 16, 1897, p. 7.

33. Abraham Hewitt, quoted in "Annual Report 1898," University Settlement, New York City, pp. 67-68.

34. Jacob Riis, in *The Playground* 8, no. 12 (March 1915): 416.

35. "Annual Reports of the Department of Parks of the City of New York, 1902, 1905."

36. *New York Times*, October 18, 1903, p. 20.

37. Ibid.

38. Ibid., October 4, 1903, p. 8.

39. Jeremy Felt, *Hostages of Fortune: Child Labor Reform in New York State* (Syracuse, N.Y.: Syracuse University Press, 1965), chap. 1.

40. Author's interview of Freida Cohen, Summer 1976.

41. Harry Roskolenko, *The Time That Was Then* (New York: Dial Press, 1971), p. 58.

42. Author's interview of Ben Levine, Summer 1976.

43. George Lukacs, *History and Class Consciousness* (Cambridge, Mass.: MIT Press, 1975), p. 78; see also, ibid., chap. 3.

44. *New York Times*, November 29, 1903, p. 15.

45. Knapp, "Parks and Politics," p. 114.

46. Thomas Brown, "The Movement for Publicly Financed Playgrounds in New York City 1890-1903" (M.A. thesis, Columbia University, 1976), p. 29.

47. Cf. "Annual Report of the Department of Education of the City of New York, 1902."

48. Roskolenko, *Time That Was*, p. 29.

49. Author's interview of Ben Levine, Summer 1976.

50. Knapp, "Parks and Politics," pp. 120-22.

51. *New York Times*, November 26, 1900, p. 1.

52. Playground Association of America, *Proceedings of the Second National Recreation Congress*, 1908, p. 335.

53. *New York Times*, December 9, 1903, p. 10.

54. Selma Berrol, "Immigrants at School: New York City 1898-1914" (Ph.D. diss., City University of New York, 1967), p. 124.

55. *New York Times*, November 25, 1903, p. 10.

56. Ethel J. Dorgan, *Luther Halsey Gulick (1865-1918)* (New York: Teachers College Press, 1934), p. 84.

57. Ibid., p. 45.

58. Ibid., p. 35.

59. *New York Times*, November 25, 1903, p. 10.

60. Ibid., August 2, 1905, p. 7.

61. Playground Association of America, "New York's Public Schools Athletic League," *The Playground* 3, no. 11 (February 1910): p. 16.

62. Berrol, "Immigrants at School," p. 124.

63. Playground Association of America, "The Public Schools Athletic League," *The Playground* no. 17 (August 1908): pp. 12-15.

64. *New York Times*, August 2, 1905, p. 7.

65. Luther H. Gulick, quoted in ibid., November 25, 1903, p. 10.

66. Luther H. Gulick, "Play and Democracy," in Playground Association of America, *Proceedings of the First National Recreation Congress*, 1907, p. 12.

67. Luther Gulick, writing in the *Annals of the American Academy of Politics and Social Science* 34 (July 1909): 40, quoted in Dorgan, *Gulick*, p. 105.

68. Gulick, "Play and Democracy," p. 12.

69. Ibid., p. 15.

70. Ibid., p. 12.

71. Author's interview of Ben Levine, Summer 1976.

72. Luther Gulick, *A Philosophy of Play* (New York: 1920), p. 254, quoted in Joel Spring, "Mass Culture and School Sports," *Quarterly Journal of Education* (Winter 1976): 488.

73. "Annual Report of the Department of Parks of the City of New York, 1914."

74. "Annual Reports of the Department of Parks of the City of New York, 1899-1913."

75. "Annual Reports of the Department of Education of the City of New York, 1898-1912."

76. "Annual Report of the Department of Parks of the City of New York, 1914."

77. "Annual Report of the Public Recreation Commission of the City of New York, 1912," pp. 1-4.

78. Samuel Haber, *Efficiency and Uplift: Scientific Management in the Progressive Era 1890-1920* (Chicago: University of Chicago Press, 1964), p. 116.

79. "The Park Question," Foreword, Part II (New York: Bureau of Municipal Research, 1908), p. 3.

80. Ibid., Part I, p. 6.

81. Ibid., Section 1.

82. Ibid., Part II, p. 4. ·

83. "Annual Report of the Public Recreation Commission of the City of New York, 1910," p. 31.

84. "Annual Report of the Public Recreation Commission of the City of New York, 1913," p. 27.

Chapter 4

1. *The Playground* 1, no. 4 (July 1907): back cover.

2. *The Playground* 10, no. 3 (June 1916): p. 92.

3. Ibid., p. 94.

4. "ORL Advocate," Box 3, p. 2. J. G. Phelps Stokes Collection, Columbia University, New York City.

5. *The Playground* 1, no. 1 (April 1907): p. 9.

6. Richard Knapp, "The National Recreation Association, 1906-1950, Part I," *Parks and Recreation* 7, no. 8 (August 1972): p. 27.

7. Playground Association of America, "The Normal Course of Play," in *Proceedings of the Third National Recreation Congress,* 1909.

8. Robert Bremner, *From the Depths* (New York: New York University Press, 1956), chap. 9.

9. Figures from the *American Jewish Yearbook,* 1914-15.

10. Playground Association of America, "Leaflet 319." National Parks and Recreation Association files.

11. Ibid.

12. Felix Warburg, in *Proceedings of the Second National Recreation Congress,* 1908, p. 203.

13. Charles F. Weller, "An Unusual Month's Work." National Parks and Recreation Association files.

14. "Early History." Miscellaneous papers in the National Parks and Recreation Association files.

15. "Field Work of L. H. Weir," p. 2. Miscellaneous papers in the National Parks and Recreation Association files.

16. Knapp, "National Recreation Association," p. 90.

17. "Field Work." Miscellaneous papers in the National Parks and Recreation Association files.

18. E. B. DeGroot, "A Practical Talk on Playground Equipment," PAA pamphlet #86, p. 4.

19. Ibid., p. 3.
20. Charles F. Weller, "School Children's Letters." Manuscript in the National Parks and Recreation Association files.
21. See *New York Sunday World,* June-September, 1905–1914.
22. "Unclassified." Miscellaneous papers in the National Parks and Recreation Association files.
23. Playground Association of America, "The Attitude of the Press Toward Play Centers," *The Playground* 9, no. 6 (September 1915): p. 189.
24. Playground Association of America, *The Playground* no. 23 (February 1909): p. 5. *New York Times* (June 21, 1903) p. 12.
25. Allen T. Burns, "The Relation of Playgrounds to Juvenile Delinquency," PAA pamphlet #30.
26. Playground Association of America, *The Playground* no. 23 (February 1909).
27. Ibid.
28. Playground Association of America, *The Playground* 3, no. 6 (September 1909).
29. Francis J. McGough "The Problems of Supervision of a Playground," *The Playground* 9, no. 4 (July 1915): 131.
30. Playground Association of America, *The Playground* 6, no. 1 (April 1912): 70.
31. Playground Association of America, "The Normal Course of Play," in *Proceedings of the Third National Recreation Congress,* 1909, "Syllabus" (hereinafter cited as "The Normal Course of Play").
32. E. B. DeGroot, "The Management of Park Playgrounds," *The Playground* 8, no. 8 (October 1914): 276.
33. "The Normal Course of Play," p. 8.
34. Playground Association of America, in *Proceedings of the Third National Recreation Congress,* 1909, p. 105.
35. John H. Chase, "How a Director Feels," *The Playground* 3, no. 4 (July 1909): 13.
36. Harry Braverman, *Labor and Monopoly Capital* (New York: Monthly Review Press, 1974), pp. 120–21.
37. Playground Association of America, "Introduction," in *Proceedings of the Third National Recreation Congress,* 1909, p. 104.
38. "Annual Report of the New York Parks and Playgrounds Association, 1913," Fieldwork.
39. George Butler, *Pioneers in Recreation* (Minneapolis: Burgess Publishing Co., 1963), p. 19.
40. Ibid., p. 26.
41. Ibid., p. 18.
42. Ibid., p. 17.
43. Ibid., p. 19; Playground Association of America, *Proceedings of the Third National Recreation Congress,* 1909, pp. 106–7.
44. Butler, *Pioneers in Education,* pp. 19–20.
45. "The Normal Course of Play," p. 126.
46. Ibid., p. 224.

47. "Annual Reports of the New York City Parks and Playgrounds Association, 1912–1914."

48. Author's interview of Ben Levine, Summer 1976.

49. Stephen A. Marglin, "What Do Bosses Do? The Origins and Function of Hierarchy in a Capitalist Production," mimeographed (Cambridge, Mass.: Harvard University; Braverman, *Labor and Monopoly Capital.*

50. "The Normal Course of Play," pp. 221–35.

51. Ibid., p. 227.

52. "Annual Report of the New York City Parks and Playgrounds Association, 1913," p. 12.

53. Ibid.

54. "The Normal Course of Play," pp. 236–37.

55. Ibid., p. 267. The playground leaders often acted as liaisons between the children's court and the immigrants.

56. Playground Association of America, *The Playground* 4, no. 3 (June 1910).

57. Butler, *Pioneers in Education,* p. 21.

58. "Annual Reports of the Department of Parks of the City of New York, 1905–1910"; "Annual Reports of the Department of Education of the City of New York, 1905–1910"; *The Playground* (1905–1910): passim.

59. Playground Association of America, *The Playground* 5, no. 1 (April 1911).

60. "The Normal Course of Play," pp. 92–93.

61. Playground Association of America, "A Brief History of the Playground Movement (cont.)," *The Playground* 9, no. 2 (May 1915): 43.

Chapter 5

1. Mark Zborowski and Elizabeth Herzog, *Life Is with People* (New York: Schocken Books, 1973), p. 38.

2. E. P. Thompson, "Time, Work-Discipline, and Industrial Capitalism," *Past and Present* 38 (December 1967): 60.

3. Harry Roskolenko, *The Time That Was Then* (New York: Dial Press, 1971), p. 62.

4. Bernard Postal, Jesse Silver, and Roy Silver, *Encyclopedia of Jews in Sports* (New York: Bloch and Sons, 1965), p. 42.

5. Irving Howe, *World of Our Fathers* (New York: Harcourt Brace Jovanovich, 1970), p. 259.

6. Postal et al., *Jews in Sports,* p. 138.

7. Abraham Cahan, "Should Children Play Baseball?" (editorial), *Jewish Daily Forward,* August 6, 1903, p. 4.

8. Playground Association of America, "The Playground Movement in America," *The Playground* 9, no. 1 (April 1915).

9. *New York Times,* August 12, 1894, p. 16.

10. *People v. Moses,* New York State Court of Appeals decision, quoted in *New York Times,* September 4, 1894, p. 9.

11. Jesse Pope, *The Clothing Industry in New York* (Columbia, Mo.: E. W. Stephens, 1905), p. 135.

12. Philip S. Foner, *History of the Labor Movement in the United States* (New York: International, 1975), 2: 19.

13. *John Swinton's Paper*, quoted in ibid., 2: 103.

14. Ibid., 2: 103.

15. Ibid.

16. Ibid.

17. According to a report by the Commission on Recreation of the City of New York completed in 1916, from 1900 to 1915 the population of children ages five to fourteen years in Manhattan increased by 75 percent.

18. G. Stanley Hall, *Youth—Its Education, Regimen and Hygiene* (New York: Appleton, 1906), p. 336.

19. John Collier, "Leisure Time, The Last Problem of Conservation," PAA pamphlet #99, p. 4.

20. *New York Times*, April 25, 1904, p. 14.

21. Joseph Lee, "Sunday Play," in Playground Association of America, *Proceedings of the Fourth National Recreation Congress*, 1910, pp. 3-12.

22. Author's interview of Charles Stein, describing his participation in May Day parades while a garment worker (1906-14), Summer 1976.

23. Foner, *History of the Labor Movement*, 2: 103-4, 115-17.

24. "The Absurdity of Personal Holidays," *The Worker*, May 1, 1903 (Special May Day issue), editorial.

25. A mammoth citywide celebration of false consciousness was sponsored by the local elite.

26. E. G. Hartmann, *The Movement to Americanize the Immigrant* (New York: Columbia University Press, 1948), p. 9.

27. Ibid., p. 42.

28. Ibid., p. 88.

29. Ibid., p. 45.

30. Ibid., p. 47.

31. Bella Mead, "The Social Pleasures of the East Side Jews" (M.A. thesis, Columbia University, 1904), p. 4.

32. Melech Epstein, *Jewish Labor in the U.S.A.* (New York: KTAV, 1969), 1: 178.

33. Author's interview of Charles Stein, Summer 1976.

34. Morris Hillquit, *Loose Leaves from a Busy Life* (New York: Macmillan, 1934), Chap. 1.

35. Pope, *The Clothing Industry*, p. 144.

36. "Annual Report of the Department of Education of the City of New York, 1910-11," p. 30.

37. "Annual Reports of the Department of Education of the City of New York, 1909-14."

38. William Maxwell, "Fourteenth Annual Playground Report," in "Annual Report of the Department of Education of the City of New York, 1911-12," p. 5.

39. "Sixteenth Annual Report on Evening Recreation Centers and Playgrounds," in "Annual Report of the Department of Education of the City of New York, 1913-14."

40. "Annual Report of the Department of Éducation of the City of New York, 1910–11," p. 27–8.

41. Selma Berrol, "Immigrants at School: New York City 1898–1914" (Ph.D. diss., City University of New York, 1967), p. 158.

42. Playground Association of America, *The Playground* 7, no. 4 (July 1913): 144.

43. "Annual Report of the Department of Education of the City of New York, 1910–11," p. 29.

44. James Weinstein, *The Decline of Socialism in America 1912–25* (New York: Monthly Review Press, 1967), chap. 2.

45. Charles Beard, *Intercollegiate Socialist* 1, no. 2 (1913) in Weinstein, *Decline of Socialism*, p. 74.

46. James Weinstein, *The Corporate Ideal in the Liberal State 1900–18* (Boston: Beacon Press, 1967), chap. 2.

47. Ibid., chap. 3.

48. Samuel Haber, *Efficiency and Uplift: Scientific Management in the Progressive Era 1890–1920* (Chicago: University of Chicago Press, 1964), p. 2.

49. Ibid., p. 65.

50. Morris Rosenfeld, "In the Shop," quoted in Epstein, *Jewish Labor*, p. 281.

51. Irwin Yellowitz, *Labor and the Progressive Movement in New York State 1897–1916* (Ithaca, N.Y.: Cornell University Press, 1965), p. 21.

52. Weinstein, *The Corporate Ideal*, p. 33.

53. Cf. Epstein, *Jewish Labor*.

54. Yellowitz, *Labor and the Progressive Movement*, p. 21.

55. See, for background, Leon Stein, *The Triangle Fire* (Philadelphia and New York: J. B. Lippincott, 1962).

56. Roskolenko, *Time That Was*, p. 58.

57. George M. Price, "The Russian Jews in America," *Publications of the American Jewish Historical Society* 48, no. 1 (1958): 50.

58. Cf. Jeremy Felt, *Hostages of Fortune: Child Labor Reform in New York State* (Syracuse, N.Y.: Syracuse University Press, 1965).

59. Contracting became an important opportunity for upward mobility; see Abraham Cahan, *The Rise of David Levinsky* (New York: Harper and Bros., 1917).

60. Pope, *The Clothing Industry*, p. 43.

61. Ibid., p. 69.

62. Abraham Cahan, *The Rise of David Levinsky* (New York: Harper and Bros., 1917).

63. "Sixteenth Annual Report on Evening Recreation Centers and Playgrounds," in "Annual Report of the Department of Education of the City of New York, 1913–14," p. 46.

64. Rose Fortune [Dorothy Richardson], *The Long Day* (New York: The Century Company, 1905), p. 104.

65. "The Normal Course of Play," p. 230.

66. C. A. Perry, "School Playgrounds," *The Playground* 4, no. 4 (July 1910);

"Annual Report of the Department of Education of the City of New York, 1910–11," p. 36.

67. Thompson, "Time," p. 82.

68. "Annual Report of the Recreation Bureau of the City of New York, 1910," p. 36.

69. Hall, *Youth*, p. 33.

70. Joseph Lee, *Play in Education* (Washington, D.C.: McGrath, 1915), p. 292.

71. Playground Association of America, *Proceedings of the Third National Recreation Congress*, 1909, p. 203.

72. Playground Association of America, *The Playground* 8, no. 5 (August 1914): 190.

73. Playground Association of America, *Proceedings of the Second National Recreation Congress*, 1908, p. 208.

74. *New York Times Magazine*, April 9, 1899, p. 4.

75. George Lukacs, *History and Class Consciousness* (Cambridge, Mass.: MIT Press, 1975), pp. 89–90.

76. Pope, *The Clothing Industry*, p. 80.

77. Roy Lubove, *The Progressives and the Slums* (Pittsburgh: University of Pittsburgh Press, 1962), pp. 94–111.

78. Howe, *World of Our Fathers*, p. 148.

79. Lubove, *The Progressives*, p. 99.

80. "Annual Report of the Recreation Bureau of the City of New York, 1910," p. 13.

81. Playground Association of America, *The Playground* no. 20 (November 1908): 11.

82. Ibid., p. 13.

83. Committee on Equipment, Playground Association of America, *The Playground* 4, no. 8 (November 1910): 274–75.

84. Lee, *Play in Education*, p. 69.

85. Hall, *Youth*, p. 94.

86. Ibid., p. 282.

87. E. B. DeGroot, "A Practical Talk on Playground Equipment," *The Playground* 5, no. 1 (April 1911): 8.

88. Helen McKintry, "Athletics for Girls," *The Playground* 3, no. 4 (July 1909): 7.

89. Playground Association of America, *The Playground* 7, no. 12 (March 1914): 482.

90. Playground Association of America, "In Memoriam—David Blaustein," *The Playground* 6, no. 9 (December 1912): 330.

91. Roskolenko, *Time That Was*, p. 15.

Chapter 6

1. Beulah Kennar, "What Playgrounds Can Do for Girls," in Playground Association of America, *Proceedings of the Second National Recreation Congress*, 1908, p. 190.

2. G. E. Johnson, "Play as a Moral Equivalent of War," *The Playground* 6, no. 4 (July 1912): 113.

3. "The Normal Course of Play," pp. 149-52.

4. G. Stanley Hall, *Youth—Its Education. Regimen and Hygiene* (New York: Appleton, 1906), p. 283.

5. Joseph Lee, *Play in Education* (Washington, D.C.: McGrath Publishing Company, 1942), p. 401.

6. Emma Goldman, Introduction, *Mother Earth* 1, no. 1 (March 1906): 11.

7. Mark Zborowski and Elizabeth Herzog, *Life Is with People* (New York: Schocken Books, 1973), pp. 247-48.

8. David Kennedy, *Birth Control in America: The Career of Margaret Sanger* (New Haven, Conn.: Yale University Press, 1970), p. 65.

9. John C. Burnham, "The Progressive Era Revolution in American Attitudes Towards Sex," *Journal of American History* 59, no. 4 (1973): 886.

10. Emma Goldman, Introduction, *Mother Earth* 1, no. 1 (March 1906): 4-10.

11. Burnham, "Progressive Era," p. 889.

12. Margaret Grant, "Modesty," *Mother Earth* 1, no. 6 (August 1906): 33-34.

13. Burnham, "Progressive Era," p. 889.

14. Emma Goldman, "The White Slave Traffic," *Mother Earth* 4, no. 11 (January 1910): 344.

15. Margaret Sanger, Introduction, *Woman Rebel* 1, no. 1 (March 1914): 1.

16. Emma Goldman, "The White Slave Traffic," *Mother Earth* 4, no. 11 (January 1910): 344.

17. *Survey.* January 22, 1910, quoted in Louis Levine, *The Women's Garment Workers* (New York: B. W. Huebsch, 1924), p. 147.

18. Thorstein Veblen, *The Theory of the Leisure Class* (Boston: Houghton Mifflin, 1973), pp. 129-30.

19. Levine, *Garment Workers*, passim.

20. Bernarr MacFadden, "Physical Culture for Boys and Girls," *Physical Culture* 3, no. 3 (1901): 157.

21. Veblen, *Leisure Class*, pp. 129-30.

22. Emma Goldman, "The Child and Its Enemies," *Mother Earth* 1, no. 2 (April 1906): 7-8.

23. "Annual Report 1902," Educational Alliance, New York, New York, p. 21.

24. Hall, *Youth*, p. 297.

25. Author's interview of Lilian Skupsky, Summer 1976.

26. See Selma Berrol, "Immigrants at School: New York City 1898-1914" (Ph.D. diss., City University of New York, 1967), esp. pp. 163-75.

27. Playground Association of America, *The Playground* 3, no. 8 (November 1909) *New York Times*, July 9, 1901, p. 7.

28. Luther Gulick, "Camp Fire Girls," *The Playground* 6, no. 6 (September 1912): 211.

29. *The Business of Home Management: The Principles of Domestic*

Engineering, quoted in Samuel Haber, *Efficiency and Uplift: Scientific Management in the Progressive Era 1890-1920* (Chicago: University of Chicago Press, 1964), p. 62.

30. The first model flat, sponsored by Mabel Kitteridge, appeared in 1902 on Henry Street. By 1907, domestic science programs were taught in 150 schools; cf. Berrol, "Immigrants at School."

31. Luther Gulick, "Camp Fire Girls,"*The Playground* 6, no. 6 (September 1912): 210.

32. Hall, *Youth,* pp. 314-26.

33. Bernard Wishy, "Images of the American Child in the Nineteenth Century" (Ph.D. diss., Columbia University, 1958), p. 239.

34. *New York Times,* April 23, 1899, p. 20.

35. Ethel J. Dorgan, *Luther Halsey Gulick (1865-1918)* (New York: Teachers College Press, 1934), chap. 1.

36. G. E. Johnson, "Play as a Moral Equivalent of War,"*The Playground* 6, no. 4 (July 1912): 113.

37. Hall, *Youth,* p. 104.

38. Playground Association of America, *The Playground* 5, no. 5 (August 1911): 370.

39. Anna L. Brown, "The Training of Recreation Secretaries,"*The Playground* 7, no. 1 (April 1913): 29.

40. Marcus Ravage, *An American in the Making* (New York: Harper Bros., 1917), p. 259.

41. Bernarr MacFadden, "The Advantages of Football," *Physical Culture* 2, no. 2 (1900): 77.

42. Abraham Cahan, Editorial, *Jewish Daily Forward,* August 6, 1903, p. 4.

43. *The Playground* 10, no. 1 (March 1916): cover.

44. G. E. Johnson, "Play as a Moral Equivalent of War," *The Playground* 6, no. 4 (July 1912): 113.

45. Joseph Lee, *Play in Education* (Washington, D. C.: McGrath Publishing Company, 1942) p. 257.

46. Miscellaneous papers, 1919-20. National Parks and Recreation Association files.

47. G. Stanley Hall, "The Question of Co-education," *Munsey's Magazine,* February 1906, p. 591.

48. Joseph Lee, *Play in Education,* pp. 407-8.

49. Hall, *Youth,* p. 284.

50. Lee Hanmer, "The Athletic Badge Test for Girls," *The Playground* 10, no. 5 (August 1916).

51. Playground Association of America, "Activities for Girls and Boys on the Playground," *The Playground* 4, no. 6 (September 1910).

52. Playground Association of America, "The Proper Relation of Organized Sports on Public Playgrounds and in Public Schools," *The Playground* 3, no. 6 (September 1909).

53. See Juliet Mitchell, *Woman's Estate* (New York: Vintage, 1973), esp. Section 2.

54. Lee, *Play in Education*, p. 394.

55. Hall, *Youth*, p. 289.

56. Hall, "Co-education," p. 591.

57. Playground Association of America, *Proceedings of the Third National Recreation Congress*, 1909, pp. 149–52.

58. *New York Times Magazine*, August 7, 1898, "Children in Central Park."

59. *New York Times Magazine*, August 31, 1904, p. 3.

60. Alexander M. Dushkin, "An Open Letter," *The Jewish Child* 2, no. 15 (May 1, 1914).

61. Hall, "Co-education," p. 592.

Chapter 7

1. Linus Kline and C. J. France, "The Psychology of Ownership," in G. Stanley Hall, *Aspects of Child Life and Education* (Boston: Ginn and Co., 1907), pp. 266–67.

2. Ibid., p. 267.

3. Karl Marx, *The Economic and Philosophic Manuscripts of 1844* (New York: International Publishers Co., 1973), p. 117.

4. Kline and France, "Ownership," p. 267.

5. Dom Cavallo, "Social Reform and the Movement to Organize Children's Play During the Progressive Era," *History of Childhood Quarterly* 3, no. 4 (Spring 1976): 510.

6. Hall, *Aspects of Child Life*, p. 247.

7. Joseph Lee, *Play in Education* (Washington, D.C.: McGrath, 1915), p. 331.

8. Cavallo, "Social Reform," p. 575.

9. James Weinstein, *The Decline of Socialism in America 1912–25* (New York: Monthly Review Press, 1967), p. 103.

10. Joseph Lee, *Constructive and Preventive Philanthropy* (Norwood, Mass.: Macmillan Co., 1902), p. 101.

11. Lee, *Play In Education*, p. 342.

12. Ibid., p. 322.

13. Ibid., p. 134.

14. Richard Knapp, "The National Recreation Association," *Parks and Recreation* 7, no. 10 (October 1972): 23.

15. Ibid., p. 24.

16. Lee, *Play in Education*, p. 134.

17. Ibid., p. 52.

18. Ibid., p. 53.

19. Ibid., p. 462.

20. Ibid., p. 54.

21. Hall, *Aspects of Child Life*, p. 25.

22. Joseph Lee, "Play as an Antidote to Civilization," Playground Association of America pamphlet #89, p. 11.

23. G. Stanley Hall, *Youth—Its Education, Regimen and Hygiene* (New York: Appleton, 1906), p. 116.

24. Ibid., p. 33.

25. Playground Association of America, "The School Playground as a National Educational Factor," *The Playground* 3, no. 5 (August 1909).

26. "The Normal Course of Play," Syllabus #4, Section A.

27. Playground Association of America, *Proceedings of the First National Recreation Congress*, 1907, p. 16.

28. "The Normal Course of Play," p. 135.

29. Playground Association of America, *The Playground* 8, no. 3 (June 1914): 104.

30. Dr. Burdick, "The Athletic Badge Test," *The Playground* 8, no. 3 (June 1914): 106.

31. Hall, *Youth*, p. 108.

32. Playground Association of America, "The Playgrounds of Endicott, Johnson and Company," *The Playground* 9, no. 3 (June 1915): 100.

33. Samuel Haber, *Efficiency and Uplift: Scientific Management in the Progressive Era 1890-1920* (Chicago: University of Chicago Press, 1964), p. 23.

34. Harry Roskolenko, *The Time That Was Then* (New York: Dial Press, 1971), pp. 82-83.

35. Benzion Liber, *The Child and the Home* (New York: Vanguard, 1927), p. 30.

36. Hall, *Youth*, p. 12.

37. Playground Association of America, *Proceedings of the First National Recreation Congress*, 1907, p. 39.

38. Seth T. Stewart, in ibid., pp. 40-41.

39. "The Normal Course of Play," p. 135.

40. Ernest Herman, "Recreation and Industrial Efficiency," *The Playground* 4, no. 10 (January 1911): 323.

41. Howard Braucher, "A Life Rather than a Living," Playground Association of America pamphlet #129, 1912-13.

42. Herman, "Recreation and Industrial Efficiency," p. 323.

43. Lee, *Play in Education*, p. 188.

44. Cavallo, "Social Reform," p. 512.

45. Joseph Lee, "Play as an Antidote to Civilization," Playground Association pamphlet #89 (July 1911): 15.

46. Lee, *Play in Education*, p. 342.

47. Hall, *Aspects of Child Life*, p. 280.

48. Ibid., pp. 248-49.

49. Marx, *Manuscripts of 1844*, p. 150.

50. Hall, *Aspects of Child Life*, p. 277.

51. Emma Goldman, "Too Little Joy," *Mother Earth* 2, no. 11 (January 1908): 513.

52. "Annual Report 1898," University Settlement, New York, New York, p. 35.

53. Ibid., p. 35.

54. Bernard Wishy, "Images of the American Child in the Nineteenth Century" (Ph.D. diss., Columbia University, 1958), p. 216.

55. Lee, *Play in Education*, p. 15.

56. Ibid., p. 244.

57. "Annual Report of the Children's Court of the City of New York, 1909," p. 7.

58. Allen Burns, "The Relation of Playgrounds to Juvenile Delinquency," Playground Association of America pamphlet #30 (1908), p. 3.

59. Ibid., p. 6.

60. Ibid., p. 5.

61. Alexander Liazos, "Class Oppression: The Functions of Juvenile Justice," *The Insurgent Sociologist* 5, no. 1 (Fall 1974): 7–8.

62. Burns, "Juvenile Delinquency," p. 5.

63. Ibid., p. 7.

64. Ibid., p. 9.

65. Ibid., p. 10–11.

66. Ibid., p. 10.

67. Liazos, "Class Oppression," p. 6.

68. Ibid., p. 19.

69. *Mother Earth* 3, no. 1 (March 1908): 10.

70. Liber, *The Child and the Home*, p. 58.

Endgame

1. Karl Marx, *The Economic and Philosophic Manuscripts of 1844* (New York: International Publishers Co., 1973), Chap. "Estranged Labor," pp. 106–19.

2. Johan Huizinga, *Homo Ludens* (Boston: Beacon Press, 1972).

3. Marx, *Manuscripts of 1844*, p. 110.

4. C. L. R. James, *Beyond a Boundary* (London: Hutchins and Co., 1963).

5. Marx, *Manuscripts of 1844*, pp. 149–50.

6. Arthur Weston, *The Making of American Physical Education* (New York: Appleton-Century-Crofts, 1962), chap. 1.

7. Henry A. Metzner, *A Brief History of the Tunerbund* (Pittsburgh: 1924).

8. Weston, *The Making*, p. 131.

9. Harry Braverman, *Labor and Monopoly Capital* (New York: Monthly Review Press, 1974), p. 90.

10. Weston, *The Making*, p. 51.

11. Marx, *Manuscripts of 1844*, p. 68.

12. Braverman, *Labor*, p. 119.

13. John Betts, *America's Sporting Heritage 1850–1950* (Reading, Mass: Addison Wesley, 1974), pp. 250–51.

14. Ibid., p. 253.

15. Marx, *Manuscripts of 1844*, p. 168.

16. "Final Report of the President's Commission on Olympic Sports" (Washington, D.C.: U.S. Government Printing Office, 1977), 1: 78–80.

17. Marx, *Manuscripts of 1844*, p. 108.

Bibliography

General History

Berrol, S. "Immigrants at School: New York City 1898-1914." Ph.D. diss., City University of New York, 1967.

Braverman, H. *Labor and Monopoly Capital.* New York: Monthly Review Press, 1974.

Bremner, R. *From the Depths.* New York: New York University Press, 1956.

Davis, A. *Spearheads for Reform: The Social Settlements and the Progressive Movement 1890-1914.* New York: Oxford University Press, 1967.

Duffy, J. *A History of Public Health in New York City 1866-1966.* New York: Russell Sage Foundation, 1974.

Felt, J. *Hostages of Fortune: Child Labor Reform in New York State.* Syracuse: Syracuse University Press, 1965.

Foner, P. *History of the Labor Movement in the United States.* Vols. 2 and 3. New York: International, 1975.

Gutman, H. *Work, Culture and Society in Industrializing America.* New York: Knopf, 1976.

Haber, S. *Efficiency and Uplift: Scientific Management in the Progressive Era 1890-1920.* Chicago: University of Chicago Press, 1964.

Hofstadter, R. *The Age of Reform.* New York: Knopf, 1956.

Josephson, M. *The Robber Barons.* New York: Harcourt Brace, 1934.

Kahn, A. J. *A Court for Children.* New York: Columbia University Press, 1953.

Kolko, G. *The Triumph of Conservatism.* Chicago: Quadrangle, 1967.

Levine, L. *The Women's Garment Workers.* New York: B. W. Huebsch, 1924.

Lubove, R. *The Progressives and the Slums.* Pittsburgh: University of Pittsburgh Press, 1962.

Nevins, A., and Krout, J. *The Greater City New York 1898-1948.* New York: Columbia University Press, 1948.

New York City Children's Court. "Annual Reports," 1903, 1906, 1909.

Park, R. and Miller, H. *Old World Traits Transplanted.* New York: Harper and Bros., 1921.

Pope, J. *The Clothing Industry in New York.* Columbia, Mo.: E. W. Stephens, 1905.

Quint, H. B. *The Forging of American Socialism.* Columbia, S.C.: University of South Carolina Press, 1953.

Ravitch, D. *The Great School Wars.* New York: Basic Books, 1974.

Richardson, J. *The New York Police.* New York: Oxford University Press, 1970.

Riis, J. *How the Other Half Lives.* New York: Hill and Wang, 1957.

Seidman, J. *The Needle Trades.* New York: Farrar and Rinehart, 1942.

Thompson, E. P. "Time, Work-Discipline and Industrial Capitalism." *Past and Present* 38 (1967)

Tyack, D. *The One Best System.* Cambridge, Mass.: Harvard University Press, 1974.

University Settlement "Annual Reports," 1894-1917.

Weinstein, J. *The Corporate Ideal in the Liberal State 1900-18.* Boston: Beacon Press, 1967.

———.*The Decline of Socialism in America 1912-25.* New York: Monthly Review Press, 1967.

Wiebe, R. *The Search for Order 1877-1920.* New York: Hill and Wang, 1967.

Yellowitz, I. *Labor and the Progressive Movement in New York State 1897-1916.* Ithaca: Cornell University Press, 1965.

Jewish Life and Culture

Adler, C. *Jacob Schiff: His Life and Papers.* New York: Doubleday, Doran, 1928.

American Jewish Yearbook, 1901, 1910, 1944.

Berkson, I. *Theories of Americanization.* New York: Teachers College Press, 1920.

Birmingham, S. *Our Crowd.* New York: Harper and Row, 1967.

Bernneimer, C. *The Russian Jew in the U.S.* Philadelphia: John C. Winston, 1905.

Blaustein, M. *Memories of David Blaustein.* New York: McBride, Nast, 1913.

Bloom, B. "Yiddish Speaking Socialists in America 1892-1905." *American Jewish Archives* 12, no. 1 (1960).

Cahan, A. *The Rise of David Levinsky.* New York: Harper and Bros., 1917.

Cantor, E. *My Life Is in Your Hands.* New York: Curtis Publishing Co., 1928.

Chotzinoff, S. *A Lost Paradise.* New York: Knopf, 1955.

Dawidowicz, L., ed. *The Golden Tradition*. Boston: Beacon Press, 1967.

Dushkin, A. *Jewish Education in New York City*. New York: Bureau of Jewish Education, 1918.

Educational Alliance "Annual Reports," 1893-1917.

———. Microfilms of Committee Reports, rolls 3-5. YIVO Collection, New York City.

———. Organizational Files. YIVO Collection, New York City.

Epstein, M. *Jewish Labor in the U.S.A.* New York: KTAV, 1969.

Feldman, W. *The Jewish Child: Its Folklore, Biology and Sociology*. London: W. M. Feldman, 1917.

Freid, J. *Jews and Divorce*. New York: KTAV, 1968.

Goren, A. *New York Jews and the Quest for Community*. New York: Columbia University Press, 1970.

Greenfeld, J. "The Role of the Jews in the Development of the Clothing Industry in the United States." *YIVO Annual of Jewish Social Science*, 2-3 (1947).

Grinstein, H. "Efforts of East European Jewry to Organize." *American Jewish Historical Society* 49, no. 2 (1959).

Hapgood, H. *The Spirit of the Ghetto*. New York: Schocken Books, 1976.

Hardman, J. B. S. "Jewish Workers in the American Labor Movement." *YIVO Annual of Jewish Social Science* 7, (1952).

Hillquit, M. *Loose Leaves from a Busy Life*. New York: Macmillan, 1934.

Jewish Child, 1912-1916.

Jewish Daily Forward, 1901-1907.

Kogut, A. "The Settlements and Ethnicity 1890-1914." *Social Work* 47, no. 1 (1972).

London, M. Personal file, available at New York University Tamiment Labor Library.

Mead, B. "The Social Pleasures of the East Side Jews." M. A. thesis, Columbia University, 1904.

Morris, R., and Freund, M. *Trends and Issues in Jewish Welfare in the U.S. 1899-1958*. Philadelphia: The Jewish Publication Society of America, 1966.

National Conference of Jewish Charities. *Proceedings*, 1902, 1904.

Ravage, M. *An American in the Making*. New York: Harper Bros., 1917.

Rischin, M. "The Jewish Labor Movement in America." *Labor History* 4, no. 3 (1963).

———. *The Promised City*. New York: Harper and Row, 1970.

Roskolenko, H. *The Time That Was Then*. New York: Dial, 1971.

Rubin, R. *Voices of a People*. New York: McGraw-Hill, 1973.

Shapiro, J. *The Friendly Society: A History of the Workmen's Circle*. New York: Media Judaica, 1970.

Shiloh, A. *By Myself I'm a Book*. Waltham, Mass.: American Jewish Historical Society, 1972.

Sklare, M. *The Jews in American Society*. New York: Behrman House, 1974.

Soltes, M. *The Yiddish Press: An Americanizing Agency*. New York: Teachers College Press, 1925.

Stein, L. *The Triangle Fire.* Philadelphia and New York: J. B. Lippincott, 1962.

Szajkowski, S. "The Attitude of American Jews to Eastern European Jewish Immigration." *Publications of the American Jewish Historical Society* 40, no. 3 (1951).

Tcherikower, E. *The Early Jewish Labor Movement in the U.S.* New York: YIVO, 1961.

Weinryb, B. "The Adaptation of Jewish Labor Groups to American Life" *Jewish Social Studies* 8, no. 4 (1946).

———. "Jewish Immigration and Accommodation." *Publications of the American Jewish Historical Society* 46, no. 3 (1957).

Wirth, L. *The Ghetto.* Chicago: University of Chicago Press. 1928.

Wolfe, G. "The Bintel Brief of the Jewish Daily Forward as an Immigrant Institution and as a Research Source". M. A. thesis, Graduate School or Jewish Social Work, 1933.

Yezierska, A. *Bread Givers.* New York: Venture, 1975.

Zborowski, M., and Herzog, E. *Life Is with People.* New York: Schocken Books, 1973.

Sport and Play

Avedon, M., and Sutton-Smith. *The Study of Games.* New York: John Wiley and Sons, 1971.

Baron, H. "Leisure-time Interests, Preferences and Activities of Children on the Lower East Side of New York City." M. A. thesis, School for Jewish Social Work, 1935.

Betts, J. *America's Sporting Heritage. 1850-1950.* Reading, Mass.: Addison Wesley, 1974.

Botkin, B. *New York City Folklore.* New York: Random House, 1956.

Brown, T. "The Movement for Publicly Financed Playgrounds in New York 1890-1903." M. A. thesis, Columbia University, 1976.

Bureau of Municipal Research. "The Park," Parts 1 and 2, New York, 1908.

Chase, J. "Street Games of New York City." *The Pedagogical Seminary* 12, (1905).

Dorgan, E. J. *Luther Halsey Gulick (1865-1918).* New York: Teachers College Press, 1934.

Edwards, H. *The Revolt of the Black Athlete.* New York: Free Press, 1970.

Geertz, C. "The Balinese Cockfight," *Daedalus* Vol. 101, no. 1 (Winter, 1972).

Gerber, E. W. *Sport and the Body.* Philadelphia: Lea and Febiger, 1974.

Goodman, C. "Degoaling Sports." *Sociology of Sport Bulletin* (Fall, 1976)

Hackensmith, C. S. *The History of Physical Education.* New York: Harper and Row, 1966.

Hall, G. Stanley. *Aspects of Child Life and Education.* Boston: Ginn and Co., 1907.

———. *Youth—Its Education. Regimen and Hygiene.* New York: Appleton, 1906.

Herron, R. E., and Sutton-Smith. *Child's Play*. New York: John Wiley and Sons, 1971.

Hoch, P. *Rip Off: The Big Game*. New York: Doubleday, 1972.

Huizinga, J. *Homo Ludens*. Boston: Beacon Press, 1972.

Kenyon, G. S. "Aspects of Contemporary Sport Sociology." CIC Symposium, Wisconsin, The Athletic Institute.

Knapp, R. "Parks and Politics: The Rise of Municipal Responsibility for Playgrounds in New York City 1887-1905." M. A. thesis, Duke University, 1968.

————. "The National Recreation Association, 1906-1950." *Parks and Recreation* 7, nos. 1, 8 & 10 (January, August, October 1972).

Lee, J. *Play in Education*. Washington, D.C.: McGrath, 1915.

Loy, J. and Kenyon, G. S. *Sport, Culture and Society*. New York: Macmillan, 1971.

Miller, D. M. *Gods and Games*. New York: Harper and Row, 1970.

New York City, Department of Education. "Annual Reports on Vacation Schools and Playgrounds," 1898-1917.

New York City, Department of Parks. "Annual Reports," 1902-1914.

New York City, Department of Parks, Public Recreation Commission. "Annual Reports," 1911-1914.

New York City, Department of Parks, Bureau of Recreation. "Annual Reports," 1910-1916.

New York City, Department of Parks, Committee on Recreation. "Annual Report," 1916.

New York City Record 41, Part 6 (June 1913).

New York Herald Tribune, 1900-1905.

New York Times, 1894-1914.

People's Institute of New York, "The City Where Crime Is Play." New York: PINY, 1914.

Physical Culture, 1899-1910.

Playground, 1907-1917.

Playground Association of America. *Proceedings of the National Recreation Congresses*, 1907-1909.

————. Pamphlets 1-100.

Postal, B.; Silver, J.; and Silver, R. *Encyclopedia of Jews in Sports*. New York: Bloch and Sons, 1965.

President's Commission on Olympic Sports. "Final Report." Washington, .C.: U. S. Government Printing Office, 1977.

D.C.: U. S. Government Printing Office, 1977.

Scott, J. *The Athletic Revolution*. New York: Free Press, 1971.

Spring, J. "Mass Culture and School Sports." *History of Education Quarterly*, no. 14 (Winter 1974).

Stokes, J. G. Phelps Collection. Columbia University, New York City.

Sutton-Smith, B. *The Folkgames of Children*. Austin: University of Texas Press, 1972.

Truxal, A. *Outdoor Recreation Legislation and Its Effectiveness*. New York: Columbia University Press, 1929.

Vincent, T. "The Political Origins of Professional Baseball." Unpublished manuscript, University of California at Berkeley, 1976.

Weston, A. *The Making of American Physical Education.* New York: Appleton-Century-Crofts, 1962.

Zucker, A. E. *The 48ers.* New York: Columbia University Press, 1950.

Theory

Aronowitz, S. *False Promises.* New York: McGraw-Hill, 1973.

Bakan, D. *Disease, Pain and Sacrifice.* Boston: Beacon Press, 1971.

Beattie, J. *Other Cultures.* New York: Free Press, 1968.

Benjamin, W. *Illuminations.* New York: Harcourt, Brace and World, 1968.

Cornforth, M. *Materialism and the Dialectical Method.* New York: International, 1972.

Davis, J. *Capitalism and Its Culture.* New York: Farrar and Rinehart, 1935.

Engels, F. *The Origins of the Family, Private Property and the State.* New York: International, 1973.

Ewen, S. *Captains of Consciousness.* New York: McGraw-Hill, 1976.

Fannon, F. *Black Skins, White Masks.* New York: Grove Press, 1968.

———. *The Wretched of the Earth.* New York: Grove Press, 1968.

Gramsci, A. *Prison Notebooks.* New York: Harper and Row, 1973.

———. *Letters from Prison.* New York: Harper and Row, 1973.

Horkheimer, M. *Critical Theory.* New York: Seabury, 1972.

———. *Eclipse of Reason.* New York: Seabury, 1974.

Horkheimer, M., and Adorno, T. W. *Dialectics of Enlightenment.* New York: Seabury, 1969.

James, C. L. R. *Beyond a Boundary.* London: Hutchins and Co., 1963.

Kerr, D. "Culture and the Streets." M.A. thesis, Columbia University, 1974.

King, R. *The Party of Eros.* Chapel Hill: University of North Carolina Press, 1972.

Kuhn, T. S. *The Structure of Scientific Revolutions.* Chicago: University of Chicago Press, 1973.

Lefebvre, H. *Everyday Life in the Modern World.* New York: Harper and Row, 1971.

Lichtman, R. "Marx's Theory of Ideology." *Social Revolution* , no. 32 (1977).

Lukacs, G. *History and Class Consciousness.* Cambridge, Mass.: MIT Press, 1975.

Marcuse, H. *Eros and Civilization.* New York: Vintage, 1955.

———. *One Dimensional Man.* Boston: Beacon Press, 1966.

———. *Negations.* Boston: Beacon Press, 1968.

———. *An Essay on Liberation.* Boston: Beacon Press, 1969.

Marx, K. *Capital,* Vol. 1. New York: International, 1970.

———. *The German Ideology.* New York: International, 1972.

———. *Grundrisse.* New York: Vintage, 1973.

———. *The Economic and Philosophic Manuscripts of 1844.* New York: International, 1973.

Poulantzas, N. *Political Power and the Social Classes*. London: NLB and SW, 1973.

Reich, W. *Sex-Pol Essays 1929–1934*. New York: Vintage, 1972.

————. *Function of the Orgasm*. New York: Touchstone, 1973.

————. *The Sexual Revolution*. New York: Farrar, Straus and Giroux, 1974.

Thompson, E. P. *The Making of the English Working Class*. New York: Pantheon, 1964.

Veblen, T. *The Theory of the Leisure Class*. Boston: Houghton Mifflin, 1973.

Williams, W. A. *The Tragedy of American Diplomacy*. New York: Delta, 1962.

Women and Children

Baum, C.; Hyman, P.; and Michel, B. *The Jewish Woman in America*. New York: Dial Press, 1976.

Burnham, J. "The Progressive Era Revolution in American Attitudes Towards Sex." *Journal of American History* 59, no. 4 (1973).

Drinnon, R. *Rebel in Paradise*. New York: Harper and Row, 1976.

Ganz, M. *Rebels: Into Anarchy and Out Again*. New York: Dodd and Mead, 1920.

Hamner, S., ed. *Women: Body and Culture*. New York: Harper and Row, 1975.

Harris, A. K. "Organizing the Unorganizable." *Labor History* 17, no. 1 (Winter 1976).

Kennedy, D. *Birth Control in America: The Career of Margaret Sanger*. New Haven, Conn.: Yale University Press, 1970.

Liber, B. Z. *The Child and the Home*. New York: Vanguard, 1927.

Mitchell, J. *Woman's Estate*. New York: Vintage, 1973.

McGovern, J. "David Graham Phillops and the Virility Impulse of Progressives." *New England Quarterly* 39, no. 3 (1966).

Mother Earth, 1906–1910.

Richardson, D. *The Long Day—The Story of a N. Y. Working Girl as Told by Herself*. New York: Century, 1905.

Sanger, M. *An Autobiography*. New York: Dover, 1971.

Schneir, M., ed. *Feminism: The Essential Historical Writings*. New York: Random House, 1972.

Index